I0436775

George W. Bush Robin Hood For The Rich

Some call you the haves and the have-mores I call you my Base, GWB October 20, 2004

by
Gene P. Abel, Colonel, USAR Ret.

Bloomington, IN  Milton Keynes, UK

authorHOUSE

AuthorHouse™
1663 Liberty Drive, Suite 200
Bloomington, IN 47403
www.authorhouse.com
Phone: 1-800-839-8640

AuthorHouse™ UK Ltd.
500 Avebury Boulevard
Central Milton Keynes, MK9 2BE
www.authorhouse.co.uk
Phone: 08001974150

© 2006 Gene P. Abel, Colonel, USAR Ret.. All rights reserved.

No part of this book may be reproduced, stored in a retrieval system, or transmitted by any means without the written permission of the author.

First published by AuthorHouse 4/13/2006

ISBN: 1-4259-2943-5 (e)
ISBN: 1-4259-2942-7 (sc)

Printed in the United States of America
Bloomington, Indiana

This book is printed on acid-free paper.

Preface

This book examines the policy changes that have taken place since George W. Bush became President of the United States. Although no amount of introspection can definitively predict the long-term impact of these policy changes, they can be examined on the basis of past events, social and economic theory and by the results and the reactions to date at home and abroad.

Regardless of how you view the way George Bush became President of the United States; no one can claim the American voters gave him a mandate for change. In November 2000 our nation was equally divided and the political atmosphere was very divisive. By 2004, in spite of President Bush's pledge to restore a more positive atmosphere to our political process, we are even more polarized and he won reelection by about 2% of the vote. It is hard to recall a time since the Civil War when the divisions in our country were more intense. The laws that have been passed since January 2001 have moved us to the right and have been designed to benefit the wealthy of America at the expense of both the middle class and the poor. The spread between the haves and the have-nots has widened and we have turned to huge increases in debt to pay for the rapidly expanding Federal budget.

The economic impact of the Bush tax cuts is clear. The poor have received no benefit since they do not pay Federal Income taxes due to their income level. In addition, the static wage rates of the low paying jobs combined with rising costs have made the plight of the poor worse over the past five years. Middle income tax payers only received any real benefit if they had children under18 or from the elimination of the marriage penalty if both adults were employed. The alternate minimum tax provisions have actually harmed many middle income tax payers. The median benefit from the Bush tax cuts for middle income Americans has been estimated at $470 per year or less then **$1.25 per day.** When President Bush proposed his tax cuts Bill Gates and Warren Buffet, the two wealthiest people on earth, wrote to Mr. Bush and advised him not to cut taxes for the wealthy. They explained to the president the wealthy did not need a tax cuts and that the country had far more pressing needs for that money. Bush ignored their advice. The Chairmen of the Federal Reserve and the Secretary of the Treasury in 2001 advised the president to tie his tax cuts to the available surplus and NOT to return to annual budget deficits. The president ignored them.

When we view consumer debt and personal savings rates the results are very clear - we are heading for trouble. The average family credit card balance has jumped from $3,300 in the mid 1990's to over $8,600 in 2005. The personal savings rate is the lowest since 1933 and in December 2005 it was negative. Americans took money out of the past savings to make purchases in December 2005. Personal bankruptcies are at an all time high. The Federal deficit, after subtracting the Social Security and Medicare surpluses of about $175 Billion, is over $400 billion in 2006. The national debt has jumped from $5.7 Trillion in January 2001 to $8.3 Trillion in January 2006. OMB has estimated the National Debt at the end of the Bush term will be about $10 Trillion and the annual interest will have jumped from **$230 Billion in 2001 to $500 Billion by 2010.**

In December 2005, David M. Walker, Comptroller General of the United States said, "The current fiscal policy is unsustainable." He went on to say, GAO simulations indicate we could be facing "rising taxes 2.5 times today's level or spending cuts of 60%." **He said that the fiscal burden that our policies have placed on Americans amounts to $350,000 for every full-time worker.**

At the same time, President Bush in his 2007 budget is proposing that his tax cuts be made permanent and the Brookings Institute released a study that shows making the tax cuts permanent will add another $2 Trillion to the national debt by 2014. Both parties selectively use statistics to justify their positions. This book will lift the fog that has been used to mask the real conditions of the United States.

On October 20, 2004 George W. Bush at a diamond–studded fund raiser in New York gave us a very clear look through the window of his soul. Mr. Bush said, "This is an impressive crowd – the haves and the have-mores. Some people call you the elites; I call you my base."

George W. Bush was not seeking the highest office in our land to be president of all the people, not even the majority, just his base –the wealthy. The policies he has implemented with the cooperation of the GOP in Congress have benefited his rich base at the expense of the middle income and poor of our country.

Table of Contents

Forward

Colonel Gene P. Abel is one of the most promising political and social commentators I have seen in recent years. He sums up many problems and issues facing the United States and the wider world in general in an informative and concise manner. He is to be applauded for a marvelous book and let us hope there are many more to come.

Sir Peter James Henry Maxwell IV

The above comments by Sir Peter Maxwell were about the Author's earlier book, Four More For George W? published in 2004.

Section one - The Impact of the Bush Policy

Economic Policy

Economic policy of the government generally falls into two areas; monetary and fiscal policy.

The Office of President has very little impact on the day-to-day monetary policy since our system has established the Federal Reserve as an independent agency. The Federal Reserve attempts to stimulate economic growth and control inflation by influencing interest rates. The Federal Reserve has done an effective job to help keep interest rates low during the past five years. This has prevented the economic downturn that began at the end of the Clinton Administration from becoming a serious recession or worse.

Federal Reserve monetary policy is directed at short-term rates but over time their policy can impact mortgage rates and the interest charged on car loans as well as credit cards.
The greatest stimulus to the economy during the past four years has been the reduction in interest rates on home mortgages. Mortgage refinancing produced more economic stimulation than all the Bush tax cuts combined.

The other issue that monetary policy attempts to control is the rate of inflation. When it looks as if inflation may be jeopardizing the economy the Federal Reserve increases interest rates to slow economic growth and the inflation that normally results from an overheated economy. During the past five years inflation has not been an issue for the economy in the United States. However, inflation is now beginning to reappear in health care, energy and food costs.

The Executive Branch wields a great deal of influence over the economy by the use of fiscal policy. The most effective actions to implement fiscal policy are government spending and tax policy.

Both these actions can have a powerful impact on economic growth and holds the potential for long-term fiscal implications.

When evaluating the Bush fiscal policy it is necessary to understand some basic economics. The economy of the United States is driven by two major factors. The more powerful factor is consumer demand that is responsible for approximately 70% of the economic activity. Capital investment or the supply side is responsible for the remaining 30%. The conservatives have argued for decades that the way to stimulate the economy is from the supply side by granting tax cuts to the wealthy that provide the capital investment for new plant and equipment in existing business and the formation of new businesses.

There are two fundamental problems with this argument. First, not all of the added money from a tax cut to the wealthy will result in capital spending. In many cases, the added wealth simply increases the portfolios of the wealthy. Second, the supply side represents the smaller component responsible for economic growth. The more powerful stimulus comes from increased consumer spending (demand). To accomplish increased consumer spending, the tax cuts need to flow to the low and middle income groups since they will spend most of the tax cuts they receive. The wealthy do not spend additional moneys produced from a tax cut. Economists have a fancy term for the spending as wealth increases called the "marginal propensity to consume". The failure of the supply side economic theory was clearly documented in the 1980's when it did not produce the rate of growth promised by President Reagan. That failure resulted in economic growth that was not sufficient to replace the lost tax revenue from the tax cuts and pay for the increased federal spending. The result was the creation of a national debt of $ 4 Trillion dollars by the end of Reagan's Presidency and a structural deficit that persisted until the last year of the Clinton Administration! By the time President Bush was inaugurated, we had a national debt of about $5.7 Trillion dollars with an annual interest payment of about $230 Billion dollars. By the time President Bush leaves office, our national debt will be in the $10 Trillion range and continuing to grow beyond 2008 by hundreds of Billions each year. That will bring our annual interest to the $500 billion dollar range which is more then the budget projections show we will be spending on national defense.

For those who cling to the validity of supply side economics, they need to explain why the largest tax cuts in recent history have failed to produce significant capital spending. The decision to invest by the wealthy once they have received their tax cut is dependent on several factors. One is the relative capacity utilization at the time they receive the additional money. During 2000 - 2003, overall industrial capacity stood at 75% utilization. That meant that, in general, we had plenty of capacity to meet additional demand without the need for new capital investment.

Another reason to invest in new capital equipment is to increase productivity. We have seen some capital spending to boost productivity, however the overall impact on the economy has not created what is required for sustained growth; job creation. Job creation is dependent on increased demand that has not responded due to the lack of added spending. In fact the increased productivity that has taken place has actually added to the lack of job creation.

The problem lies in the philosophy of the conservatives that the money should be returned to the people who pay it. Certainly if we look at who pays a large portion of the income taxes, a strong argument can be made for the kinds of tax cuts George Bush has pushed through Congress. However, if the objective is to achieve the most effective way to stimulate the economy than we have taken the wrong approach. More than 400 of the nation's leading economists tried to tell Bush this when he proposed his tax cuts. They took a full-page ad in the Wall Street Journal to emphasize their point. The Federal Reserve Chairman advised President Bush against the form of tax cuts he proposed and the former secretary of the Treasury, Paul O'Neill did not support the second and third Bush tax cuts. It is clear that at the present time, world events have created a need to fund our security at a rate that was far higher than since the Reagan years. We justified the debt that resulted from the Reagan tax cut and Reagan spending by the peace dividend from running the Soviet Union out of business.

Time has however shown us that what we really did is change the nature of the threat to our country, not reduce the danger. The Soviet Union was a powerful but predictable adversary. They exerted a level of control over the radical Muslim factions that are creating many of our current security problems. When the Soviet Union disappeared, this control ended and allowed these groups to strengthen their organizations and to move forward with their objectives.

The United States began to use this peace dividend during the first Bush Administration when Secretary of Defense Cheney laid out a plan to reduce the military. President Clinton took this process even further and the result is that we do not have the intelligence gathering capability or military needed to meet the current security threat. In fact the Clinton administration did not even replace many of the munitions used in the first Gulf War.

The result of the peace dividend and the reduced military spending culminated in three years of budget surpluses after almost two decades of deficits. The policy being followed by the Bush administration is to increase spending in some areas while ignoring other requirements such as education and some aspects of homeland defense. Concurrent with the added spending George Bush has cut taxes to the point of significantly adding to the annual budget deficit. Now Mr. Bush is trying to make these tax cuts permanent despite his budget projections that never produce a balanced budget.

This has brought us to a situation where we have the worst of both worlds. We have lost substantial amounts of federal revenue from the tax cuts at a time when our expenditures are rapidly growing. We need to understand for every dollar that is lost from a tax cut the economy needs to grow by four dollars to just offset the loss in the federal revenue. In other words if we cut taxes by $100 billion dollars per year the economy needs to add $400 billion in taxable income from growth because the average tax rate is about 25%. Economists call this the multiplier effect.

The problem we are faced with is that the economic growth from the Bush tax cuts has been only marginally effective. We have not seen the huge capital investments that he said would result from the supply side economic theories. It is likely this is due in part to the reluctance of businessmen to believe the economic growth will continue. In addition our excess capacity needs to be utilized before businesses are willing to commit additional monies for capital expansion to increase capacity.

During the past five years, our economy should have produced six million new jobs to keep pace with the growing population. During the past five years the economy has added about 4.5 million jobs. Thus, the consequences of the economic downturn in the early part of the Bush presidency and the lack- luster economic growth resulting from the Bush economic policy has resulted in a shortfall of 1.5 million jobs. We were told that the tax cuts would stimulate the economy and return our economy to a growth status. We have seen some increases in productivity, profits, and the stock market. However, without creating jobs to provide disposable income to working Americans, we cannot produce a meaningful and sustainable recovery. Many of the jobs that are being created are paying a small fraction of the jobs we are losing. Statistically, it looks as if we are making progress but the fact is there is a vast difference between losing a job paying $20 an hour and creating another paying $10 an hour. The Bush administration points to the drop in the unemployment rate. This is a clever use of statistics. The truth is that so many people have been unemployed for so long they are no longer being counted as unemployed. If we counted these people, the "real" unemployment rate would be far above the official rate cited by Bush. The net result of the tax policies employed have added to the Federal deficit and failed to produce the level of economic growth needed to move us toward a balanced budget.

The employment numbers for February 2005 were a step forward by producing 262,000 new jobs. Not only is that more than were expected, but it is more than economists claim are necessary to keep pace with population growth. To keep pace with our growing work force, our economy needs to produce about 125,000 new jobs each month. Thus, last month we produced more than double that amount. Most would believe that would result in a reduction of the nation's unemployment rate when in fact the unemployment rate increased from 5.2 to 5.4%.

We have seen months in the past when almost no jobs were created and the unemployment rate went down. Thus it is clear, t he unemployment rate statistic is not giving us a clear picture of job condition in our country. What we should be doing is producing monthly, the number of Americans who do not have jobs that pay a living wage. It should include all people who need a living wage job that do not have such a job and compare that statistic month-to-month see how well we are doing in creating meaningful jobs for our growing population.

Staff members at the Bureau of Labor, Division of Labor Statistics said, "the official unemployment rate doesn't provide a full picture of labor market difficulties". They suggested looking at labor underutilization U-6 table A-12. They indicated that includes those who are underemployed (jobs that do not generally pay a living wage). These rates, which are the broadest measure of workers that do not have jobs that provide a living wage, are" twice that of the official unemployment rate".

In January 2006, The U. S. Conference of Mayors, a non-partisan group, released the results of the U.S. Metro Economies 2004-2005 Report. Here are a few of the Key Findings from that report:

Labor markets across the country have not regained the jobs lost (numbers) in the 2001 -2002 recession.

At the end of 2005, 18 states had not recovered their job losses.

The jobs that have been created in 2004-2005 **pay 21% less** then the jobs lost in 2001-2003.

The study documented that the average annual wage of the jobs lost during the three years was $43,629 compared with $34,378 for the jobs created during 2004 and 2005.

Many of these new jobs also provided far less benefits, especially for health and retirement.

These results show the impact of the economic recovery on the average American more accurately then GDP growth, increased corporate profits or productivity increases. Even if we had replaced all the job loss, after accounting for the new workers that entered the work force since January 2001, if they pay 1/5 LESS, we do not have anything like an economic recovery to the people who have these newly created jobs. This also impacts the overall dollars that these workers have to spend in the economy. The quality of newly created jobs in terms of pay and benefits MUST be considered when evaluating the real impact of the economic recovery.

When we turn our attention to the financial condition of individuals in the United States we find that the amount of consumer credit outstanding is about two trillion dollars which is an all-time high. The conservatives tell us it's not important when you consider inflation. However, the validity of that argument fades when you factor in the number of personal bankruptcies that are also at all-time high in 2005. This will also give us a clearer picture as to the ability of individuals to continue spending. The consumer either pays for consumption with cash or credit. When both are in short supply it does not paint a rosy picture for sustained spending much less increased demand. Since the average consumer is not receiving large amounts from the Bush tax cuts and is carrying increasing amounts of debt, added spending is unlikely. Add the lack of job creation and the economic outlook is weak at best.

There is another area that the Bush Administration has totally ignored and that is the need to rebuild our infrastructure. President Bush seems to understand this principal when it comes to Iraq since he convinced Congress to spend another $21 billion to rebuild their infrastructure. There are estimates that put the infrastructure repairs needed in the United States at more than $1 trillion dollars. In some cases the urgency of these repairs is very high for things such as our dams and electrical grid. The nation's schools, according to the 1996 GAO report, require more than $115 billion worth of repairs. This amount does not touch the needs for new school construction due to the surge in student growth. The failure of the levies surrounding New Orleans during Katrina is an example of what ignoring the repair of America's infrastructure will cost us in the future. There is NO movement by the Bush administration and the conservatives in Congress to tackle the needs to repair America. They can only spend American Tax money to help rebuild Iraq while turning a deaf ear to our needs!

State and local governments do not have the funding to make these capital improvements given the added burden that they have today from homeland defense. If the Bush administration was truly interested in a fiscal policy that would maximize the rate of return to the country rather than just helping his wealthy contributors, we would take the money from the tax cuts for the top two income brackets and the elimination of the Estate Tax and invest it in our country. The impact of spending these federal tax dollars to rebuild our infrastructure would be far more effective in providing economic growth by putting people to work. It would produce profits to the companies doing the work that would create a need for more capital investment and produce increased corporate profits. When we have completed this investment our country would then have the new facilities needed to support our nation for decades to come. Compare that alternative with providing tax cuts to the ultra wealthy. Does anyone believe under the Bush policy the wealthy will step up and offer to rebuild our schools, roads, bridges, dams etc.? Under the Bush policies, how will we rebuild this country's infrastructure? Some may offer the rationale that the wealthy will buy tax-exempt bonds to rebuild the infrastructure. The only problem with this solution is, where does the money come from to repay the bonds? If we use the money from the tax cuts to the wealthy, there are no bonds to repay.

A look at the Office of Management and Budget (OMB) summary of the Bush budget projections shows a total indifference toward fiscal sanity. As Mr. O'Neill stated, the attitude of the Bush Administrations officials toward the growing national debt is that it does not matter. As proof they sighted what took place under President Reagan. In 2008 the Bush budget projection shows the United States running a deficit of $200 billion with a total national debt of just under $10 Trillion. This compares with a national debt in 2000 of $5.7 trillion. Note this is if the economic growth that Mr. Bush assumed in his budget materializes.

The final budget deception is that even the President's projected deficit of $10 Trillion by 2008 is understated by trillions of dollars. The reason the actual deficit is understated is because the budget deficit is calculated using an accounting trick called the "Unified Budget".

The unified budget combines the Federal Budget with Social Security and Medicare. At the present time, both Social Security and Medicare show an annual surplus. They both collect more in taxes then they pay out in benefits. This will come to an end as the baby boomer retirements increase.

In 2003, a comparison of the deficit using the Unified Budget calculation with the Federal Budget, without Social Security and Medicare, was completed using data from the Congressional Budget Office by the Center For Economic And Policy Research. It clearly showed the impact of combining Social Security and Medicare with the Federal Budget. In 2003, the deficit reported by the Bush administration, using the Unified Budget method, showed a deficit of $400 Billion. Looking only at the Federal Budget, the 2003 deficit was $600 billion. The actual budget deficit without counting the Social Security and Medicare surplus was over $500 billion in FY2005.

The study concluded that the tax cuts left the budget seriously out of balance and calculated what it would require in spending cuts or tax increases to bring the 2003 budget into balance without Social Security and Medicare. To balance the 2003 Federal Budget alone would require **spending cuts of 36.1%** or **tax increases of 56.6%.**

The only reason to distort the true federal deficit by adding the surpluses from Social Security and Medicare is to make the deficit appear smaller. When Social Security and Medicare no longer are generating an annual surplus, the true size of the Federal Budget Deficit will become clear. This process is like combining the financial statements of three companies, the first with very large losses with two others that each a show small profits to reduce the size of the loss in first company. If President Bush had to certify the financial statements of the Federal Budget, the way corporate CEO's are required today, he would be in violation of the law. It is too bad that this law does not apply to the CEO of our nation.

The Bush budget in 2008 will be spending more on interest than for defense and more on interest than for all non-defense discretionary spending! Interest payments do nothing to meet the needs of our country; they pay for prior year's irresponsible fiscal policy. We are placing a terrible burden on the future generations because we refuse to act in a responsible way. If we wind up with another four years of the current policy, the task of restoring fiscal sanity to our federal budget will be very difficult. If we are faced with similar security issues in the future and given the demands the retirement of the baby boomers will impose on the budget, we will have little choice than to impose sizeable tax increases to remain solvent.

The current policies of the conservatives are clearly charge and spend. Much of the spending given our security situation is unavoidable. It is ongoing and to think that we can reduce spending is unrealistic. The reality is that spending will most likely increase faster then the rate of inflation. Should a terrorist organization again inflict another tragedy on our country, the economic fallout will further complicate our financial problems. To face such a prospect given the current deficit and the continued expectation of ongoing deficits is the wrong policy. We should be running a surplus so as to have a cushion should another tragedy befall us.

There is one theory, voiced by Professor Paul Krugman at Princeton that conservatives are attempting to create a fiscal crisis by cutting taxes while continuing to spend. Those who support this idea believe that when it is clear we can no longer meet our obligations, the conservatives will offer a solution of either eliminating or substantially cutting both Social Security and Medicare. It is a long-held belief that the conservatives dislike both of these social programs and would like to either reduce them in scope or eliminate them altogether. In reality, these two programs are among the most popular social legislation ever enacted by Congress. For anyone either close to retirement or retired, the prospect to curtail or eliminate either Social Security or Medicare, could produce a backlash that could unseat the conservatives from power. The resulting shift in power could produce a solution to the fiscal crisis by drastically increasing the tax burden on the wealthiest Americans. Increasing the tax on the highest-paid Americans and extending Social Security tax to include all earned income are but two of the possible alternatives that might be imposed to fully fund Social Security and Medicare.

At the beginning of this section the impact of the low interest rates on our economy was discussed. The continuation of low interest rates will be difficult given the federal deficit. As the Federal Reserve borrows more and more to fund the growing debt, the pressure on interest rates to rise will be unstoppable. However, if the net result of the huge federal deficits is an increase in interest rates, the driving elements of our economy will be adversely impacted. Increases in the interest rates on mortgages and car loans will slow the growth in the economy. Therefore the very policy of charge and spend that President Bush is following may be his undoing. The increase in short term interest rates by over 3% has begun to show in long term rates with 30 year fixed mortgage rates increasing from below 5% in 2003 to just over 6% in the fall of 2005.One of the fundamental problems the Bush administration is faced with is that the spending increases are not for pork barrel projects but rather essential government services. For years we heard from the conservatives that we need to cut spending. The Bush administration has not argued that concept given the fact that so much of the spending increases deal with issues that most voters consider essential. Even with the substantial spending increases that we have seen during the past four years, there are major areas that are simply not being funded at adequate levels. Things such as protecting our borders, inspecting shipping containers and cargo planes, and an active military capable of meeting the assignments it has been given, public education and the "no child left behind act" are but a few of the areas which require increased federal spending.

Our tax laws are more complex than they have ever been and with each of the Bush tax cuts yet another layer of complexity have been added. We need to simplify our tax structure as well as bring our tax revenue into line with our spending. The Bush Administration does not seem to be willing to provide the government services that the majority wants the federal government to provide and be willing to pay for them.

There is an old saying; those who fail to learn from history are destined to repeat it. With the exception of the high interest rates during the Reagan Administration, the tax and spend policies of the Bush Administration are almost identical to the Reagan Administration. In 1980 candidate Reagan promised the American people if his tax cuts were approved we would have a balanced federal budget by 1985. Not only did we not balance the budget with the Reagan tax cuts but we continued ever increasing deficits which culminated in the roughly $4 trillion of national debt when Reagan left office. What makes anyone believe that current policy of trickle-down supply side economics would produce a better result than it did in the 1980's? In just four short years the Bush policy has produced almost the same increase in the debt as President Reagan.

The logic used by the Bush administration for its tax cuts was that the rate of tax on the wealthy was oppressive. When we look at the boom of the 1990s, the economic group that did the best was the wealthy.

How then were the wealthy able to do so well with the oppressive tax rates that were in place prior to the Bush tax cuts? Another argument used by President Bush to justify cutting federal taxes is that it prevents the Congress from spending money they do not have. By the end of 2003, Congress managed to spend an additional $87 billion in Iraq without identifying any way to pay for this additional expenditure. Congress, at the urging of President Bush, passed a prescription drug benefit under Medicare that will add $550 billion to the federal budget over the next 10 years. Where is this money to come from? Therefore the argument that Congress cannot spend the money if they cut taxes has been proven to be false.

Given the current need to fund our security, social needs, costs associated with population growth, and the cost the baby boomers will impose on the federal budget, we need to maximize our economic growth. Unfortunately the Bush economic policy is not producing a level of growth necessary to fund the needs of our country.

Since the objective of this book is to provide some insight into the likely consequences of the Bush policy changes, we need to outline the economic outlook for the future. In the near term, we should see further improvement in the economy given the fact that the federal government is gorging the economy with a half trillion dollars of deficit spending. Normally such a policy would be followed as a pump priming exercise when we are in deep recession. However, today what we are doing is paying for essential additional spending with this debt. We should see continued growth in the Gross Domestic Product (GDP), increases in productivity, as well as modest job creation. The stock market should continue its upward trend until the point when interest rates begin to rise. At that point the party on Wall Street will most likely come to end.

The long-term reality of the Bush economic policy is that it will not provide for the funding needed to pay for our basic necessities. It will not provide the federal revenue to fully fund our security, meet our obligations to the baby boomers as they retire, educate the record number of school-age children, and repair the decaying infrastructure in the United States. The amount of growth that would be required to produce the needed federal revenue after the Bush tax cuts to fund all of these requirements is unrealistic. President Bush does not intend to balance the budget, rebuild the infrastructure of this country or solve the Social Security and Medicare funding issues.

The day is coming when will be forced to face the reality that our economic policy has not produced the needed tax revenue to pay our bills. By ignoring things such as the national debt, the need to fund Social Security and Medicare, and the repair of our infrastructure, we are setting ourselves up for a very painful reality.

The next generation will be saddled with the consequences of what we are doing today. They will be faced with either cutting essential government services or accepting staggering increases in the rate of taxation to balance the budget. Because these issues are so basic, it is difficult to believe that the majority of the population would accept the magnitude of cuts that would be required to balance the budget through spending cuts. The more likely scenario is that the majority will insist the federal government continue providing these services and increase the tax burden. The result could be a 50% tax rate on the middle-income Americans and tax rates on the wealthy that we have not seen since before the Reagan tax cuts in the 1980s. This would place Americans in the same situation as many of our allies in Europe.

All these projections are predicated on not experiencing another terrorist incident equal to or worse than 9/11. Should this country experience yet another devastating attack, the economic consequences become even direr. Given the world situation we should be in a position of having a budget surplus with little or no national debt. If the issues requiring funding were not so large or so essential, solutions to the fiscal imbalance of today would be much simpler to solve. The truth is that the funding requirements are both **essential and sizable**. When you add the cost of the various under or unfunded needs that we are facing, the total is staggering. Therefore, the legacy of the Bush fiscal policy will fall to the next generation. When the day comes that we can no longer ignore our responsibilities and we simply do not have the federal revenue to meet those responsibilities, we will then be faced with the ugly reality, which will be the shameful legacy of George W. Bush and his fiscal agenda!

National Defense

During the campaign of 2000, Bush seemed to understand we had overused the so-called peace dividend and that our military, especially the Army, was too small. Bush also campaigned on a belief that the United States should limit its actions in nation building. It is hard to know whether Mr. Bush recognized the shortcomings in our security services that suffered from a lack of human resources and collaboration among the various agencies. Clearly the events of 9/11 documented in spades that we were vulnerable to attack and our intelligence network was inadequate.

From the outset, President Bush ignored what he said during the campaign. First were his plans to invade and occupy Iraq (nation building). The evidence is clear Mr. Bush was doing more than just maintaining a policy that said we would like to see a regime change in Baghdad. The Pentagon began preparing war plans to both invade and occupy Iraq and the political discussions began in the Cabinet meetings soon after Mr. Bush's election. Secretary O'Neill, in the book The Price of Loyalty stated that discussions began during the first month of the Bush administration to invade and occupy Iraq. Perhaps part of Mr. Bush's motivation all along was to seek revenge for the assassination attempt on his father by Saddam Hussein and to help with his own reelection.

At the same time the Bush White House was planning the Iraq adventure, the Secretary of Defense set aside the issue of expanding our military strength. Instead Secretary Rumsfeld began his campaign to restructure the Department of Defense. It is true that the nature of the threat facing the United States has significantly changed since the end of the Cold War. Restructuring the military, to better align itself with the new threat, is a legitimate undertaking.

However, restructuring alone does not deal with the adequacy of the active component to accomplish its mission. During the Cold War the United States faced an enemy of immense power that was relatively predictable. Today we face a combination of rogue states and international terrorist organizations such as al-Qaeda that have the capability of employing weapons of mass destruction (WMD). However, the real danger comes from the militant Islamists as Michael Scheuer points out is his book, Imperial Hubris.

The Bush defense policy has concentrated only on reorganizing our military assets without considering the deficiency in our military resources. The number of deployments to confront the ever-expanding nature of the threats against us has stretched the military, especially the Army and Marine Corps, to the breaking point. In December of 2003, the Army War College published an issue paper entitled "Balancing the Force" which acknowledges the current problems experienced by over-utilization of the Reserve and National Guard components of our defense establishment. It however failed to address the issue of the inadequacy of the active component that has caused extended deployments of both Reserve and National Guard units. The consequences are beginning to surface in that National Guard and Army Reserve units are unable to meet their recruiting and retention goals. Many Reservists and Guardsmen are leaving their assignments upon returning from Iraq. The Defense Department has turned to a variety of methods to provide the necessary force levels to rotate units from Iraq. Stop-loss orders preventing members from retiring for up to one and a half years beyond their planned retirement have been employed. This is only a stopgap measure and does not address the need to increase the active component of the military. Most senior military leaders admit that we can not sustain a troop level of 150,000 in Iraq during 2006 without an all out Reserve and National Guard mobilization or by sending troops on 3rd or even 4th tour in Iraq. In November 2005, 2/3 of Americans now want an end to the U S adventure in Iraq and Bush will most likely be forced to lower the troop levels before the Congressional elections in November 2006.

The rotation that began in early 2004, utilized 40,000 more National Guard and Reserve forces because the active component does not have the wherewithal to relieve the assigned units at the end of their 12-month tour of duty. The long-term consequences of failing to provide sufficient active military strength to meet the ever-increasing deployments are very risky.

Why the Bush administration failed to increase the military is most likely due to the added cost. The Bush tax cuts seem to have a higher priority than national defense. Again the reelection motivation comes to mind.

A prime consequence of not providing the needed military strength is what happened in Iraq after the military's brilliant defeat of Saddam Hussein. The first pictures America saw after the defeat of the military forces in Iraq were riots and lawlessness in the streets of Iraq. Bush and Rumsfeld insisted there were sufficient numbers of troops to control the situation in Iraq. It soon became clear this was not the case. The 130,000 US troops plus the roughly 20,000 British troops could not deal with the several hundred thousand former members of the Iraq military who melted into the civilian population and became a source of guerrilla insurgency. The available troops were unable to secure the borders of Iraq and prevent the infiltration of terrorist groups from all over the Middle East. In addition, they were unable to safeguard the water, electric and petroleum facilities in Iraq. Scores of ammunition dumps remain unguarded and are providing the source for the explosives being used to kill Americans in Iraq day-after-day.

When the former Army Chief of Staff, General Eric Shinseki provided his assessment that it would take several hundred thousand boots on the ground to secure the peace in Iraq, the President and Secretary of Defense told us he was wrong. It was the President and Secretary of Defense that did not understand the nature of the problem. The lack of manpower has caused frustration from the Iraqis and has produced additional casualties to both the United States and its coalition partners. Because of the Bush policy toward the United

Nations and countries that did not agree with our going to war, we were unable to obtain assistance from other nations to secure Iraq.

The issue of the Army strength is gaining steam. In the past, active duty general officers have been reluctant to come forward because Rumsfeld and his aides are well known for harshly dealing with anyone who dissents. However, in an interview in The Sun, Lt. General John M. Riggs, and a decorated Vietnam veteran who is in charge of building the Army of the future has come out indicating we need at least 80,000 more active Army troops. Rumsfeld is not giving up on his opposition to expanding the Army. He ruffled the feathers of the top Army brass when he coaxed Retired General Peter J. Schoomaker to take over as the Army Chief of Staff. Schoomaker is one of the few senior officers that agree with Rumsfeld about not increasing the Army strength which puts him at odds with Lt. General Riggs.

Retired General Barry McCaffrey has also suggested that the Army needs to be increased by 80,000 troops. It appears most of the senior military officers understand the Army must be increased. The issue for Rumsfeld is the added cost of about $1.2 Billion per year for each 10,000 added end strength. He insists, the added cost would have to be taken from other areas of the Defense budget. It is time to apply the same solution Mr. Rumsfeld employed for the added money for Iraq and increase the Defense appropriation. Congress is now becoming aware of the need for a larger Army and 150 members of Congress support a larger Army. It is time to remind the Secretary of Defense that it is Congress that is responsible to set the end strength of the military and approve the budget.

The policy change raised by the preemptive use of our military is a major issue. The specter of the world's most powerful nation using its immense military power to unseat another government is unnerving to many other countries. The only justification most world leaders would accept for such action would be to prevent an imminent attack. Since it is clear the United States was not in any such danger from Saddam Hussein, our actions cannot be considered as justified.

From the outset of his administration, President Bush insisted the United States develop a missile defense system. Neither the huge cost nor treaty complications would deter Bush from developing this system. The type of missile defense system being developed by the Bush administration employs sophisticated radar and computer systems in an attempt to destroy an incoming missile with an intercept missile launched from within the United States.

This system has several fatal flaws. First is the issue of reliability. During the first series of tests almost half of the time it failed to destroy the incoming missile. The estimated cost to deploy the system is over $100 billion dollars that does not include the ongoing cost to operate the system when it is operational. All of this however does not address the most important shortcoming of the Bush missile defense system, which is **the lack of benefit from the system**. There are almost no rogue states that have the capability of launching a nuclear weapon at the United States. In addition should a rogue state obtain a missile and nuclear warhead capable of attacking our nation, the second it lifted from its launch pad the rogue state would be history? Any and every tyrant that would think of using such a weapon against the most powerful nation on earth would be committing suicide. Therefore we are building a weapon system that will provide almost no real protection to the United States since the likelihood of fending off an attack by a rogue state is almost nonexistent. The Bush administration admits its missile defense system is not designed to destroy large numbers of missiles, and therefore does nothing to defend us against Russia or China.

The real danger from nuclear weapons and other weapons of mass destruction is from terrorist groups bringing them into this country on planes or in shipping containers. More than three years after 9/11 we are still not inspecting shipping containers or cargo planes coming in to our nation. We seem to be able to find $100 billion dollars to build a nearly useless missile defense system but we don't have the money to provide the manpower to inspect what comes in to our country.

If we are looking to develop a space-based weapon system, we need to concentrate on the high-energy laser systems not the bullet-to-bullet type anti missile systems being developed by Bush. Laser systems have the capability of attacking targets in the air, on the ground and on the water. In addition, they have the ability to be fired multiple times should the initial use fail to destroy the target. The system that Bush is spending $100 billion on is a one-shot deal. If that intercept missile fails to hit the enemy missile, we have no effective defense. Also, its use is limited to other missiles.

After 9/11, the American people were faced with the reality that we were not safe from attack. Terrorist incidents that took place in other countries had now come to New York and Washington. The Bush administration did not cause these terrorist attacks, however it is clear that they do not fully understand the nature of the danger facing us.

In December 2003, Jeffery Record a visiting professor at the Army War College published a highly critical paper concerning the lack of understanding by the Bush administration of the threat facing America. Professor Record made some very perceptive points in his article. First, President Bush has incorrectly lumped al-Qaeda and Saddam Hussein's Iraq into a "single undifferentiated terrorist threat." According to Professor Record, this was a "strategic error of the first order because it ignored critical differences between the two in character, threat level and susceptibility to U.S. deterrence and military action." He went on to say, "The result has been an unnecessary preventive war of choice against a deterred Iraq that has created a new front in the Middle East for Islamic terrorism and diverted attention and resources away from securing the American homeland against further assault by an undeterrable al-Qaeda. The war against Iraq was not integral to the GWOT (global war on terrorism) but rather a detour from it."

Professor Record goes on to say that the Bush policy fails to understand a different nature of terrorism from groups like al-Qaeda and rogue states such as Iraq, Iran and North Korea. He pointed out, the United States has never been attacked by a rogue state and the danger from rogue states is very different than from terrorist groups. The reason lies in what each has to lose by their actions. Terrorists operate within an existing country and as such are not subject to large military action. They do not have a country to lose, just a relatively few number of followers and one of many bases of operation. Therefore, attacks like 9/11 will continue to be attempted by terrorist organizations that are at odds with the U.S. Rogue states will be much more careful and limited in the options available to them. It is true, the preemptive use of our military and the willingness of Bush to go it alone has and will help restrain the actions of rogue states even though it violates our long-standing policy that has made us so effective in world diplomacy in the past. It will not have any significant impact on restraining groups such as al-Qaeda or the terrorists groups opposing Israel. The most significant short-coming with the Bush vision is that he fails to understand these differences and direct our response in the most effective way. Professor Record believes this is a major policy flaw with the Bush administration. He also made it clear that we do not have sufficient resources to engage every terrorist organization throughout the world. In addition, there are many terrorist organizations that do not pose a threat to the United States. Attacking such groups would squander our resources and help create more enemies.

Professor Record also points out some reasons why groups such as al-Qaeda and the terrorists fighting Israel are so willing to give up their lives. He states that, "terrorism is recourse of the politically desperate and military helpless." Terrorists do not consider themselves doing things that are wrong but rather that are necessary to achieve their objectives. We can certainly disagree with their justification for their terrorist acts, but the fact remains there are millions of these individuals who are committed to their belief. We see this when Israel retaliates after a terrorist attack. Did the attacks stop or did they create a whole new group of individuals willing to die in order to kill more Israelis? It's a cycle that is not producing a solution. The Iraq War has created a focal point for many of the terrorist organizations to attack the coalition forces and frustrate our attempts to restore order in Iraq. Saddam Hussein was not a terrorist per se and the existence of international terrorist groups was not an issue in Iraq before the war. It is a painful consequence of the failure by President Bush to understand the differences between how we can effectively deal with international terrorist groups and the evil dictators of rogue states.

All of us remember the graphic example cited by the Vice President when he stated that we could not wait for the smoking gun in Iraq because it might be a mushroom cloud over one of our cities. This was clearly an attempt by the Bush Administration to convey to the Congress, the American people, and the world that we were facing a possible nuclear attack from Saddam Hussein. It is clear that Iraq did not pose any such threat to the U.S. from nuclear weapons. Unless we are able to uncover meaningful stockpiles of biological or chemical weapons in Iraq, there was no real danger to the United States from the Iraqi dictator. As Professor Record points out in his paper, we had diverted our attention by attacking Iraq who did not pose a serious threat to our nation. The revenge leitmotif is heard again. In doing so we fail to address the greater danger that is posed by the terrorist organizations that operate throughout the world. We sent about 6,000 American troops to Afghanistan where 9/11 was planned and 130,000 of our troops to Iraq to depose Saddam Hussein who did not pose nearly the threat that Osama bin Laden posed. There is no doubt that Saddam Hussein was a tyrant who did not deserve to be the leader of the Iraqi people. However it is not the responsibility of the United States to liberate every group of people who is dominated by a despot like Hussein (doctrine of preemption). In fact there are dictators in this world who have killed even more people than Saddam Hussein and who pose a much greater threat to this country, e.g. the leaders of North Korea. At this point we cannot walk away from Iraq without establishing a government capable of preventing a civil war. The question that only time can answer is, what type of government will emerge in Iraq? We may find what replaces Saddam Hussein will not be to our liking.

The policy shift that we have seen in the Bush administration by the preemptive use of our military is a serious issue that needs to be debated by the Congress. I wonder how many Congressmen and Senators would have voted for the war resolution if they had the facts available today. There was no direct connection to the attacks on the United States on 9/11 from Iraq and there was no WMD found. . The nuclear weapons program in Iraq was non existent and the mushroom cloud the Vice President Cheney emphasized in his speech was just another attempt to distort the danger from Saddam. In addition, Iraq was not attempting to purchase uranium as President Bush claimed in his State of the Union address and there were no mobile chemical labs as General Powell claimed in his fabricated U N Speech on Feb 5, 2003.

The rationale that is now being embraced for the Iraq War is that the people of Iraq need to be liberated from their evil dictator and that we had to enforce the UN resolutions which Saddam Hussein clearly ignored. The problem with this rationale is that Saddam Hussein is one of many tyrants that exist in the world today. Is the United States to liberate all people who live under tyrannical rule? When did the United Nations appoint the United States and Great Britain as the enforcement agent for the Security Council resolutions? It was the responsibility of the UN, not the United States or Great Britain to enforce the UN resolutions.

The Bush supporters try to justify his actions by asking if we would rather see Saddam Hussein in power. The answer to that is obviously, NO! However, placing the United States military at risk and spending hundreds of billions of tax dollars to remove a bad man from Iraq should not be the policy of the United States. It can be rationalized to use our military power in a preemptive fashion if it is to truly protect America. There is no evidence that Iraq posed such a danger to the people of the United States and therefore the policy decision to attack Iraq was unjustified. It has set a very dangerous precedent.

Only George Bush knows when he finally decided to attack Iraq. However, statements by General Clark and Secretary O'Neill indicate that this took place prior to 9/11 and was part of his agenda from the beginning of his administration. Whether or not the intelligence was inaccurate is the question that needs to be evaluated to ensure that we are able to protect ourselves in the future. There is little doubt that President Bush manipulated the intelligence to justify the predetermined policy of regime change chosen from the outset of his administration. Bush ignored any intelligence that suggested his rational for attacking Iraq was not justified. What we know in 2005 is that much of the intelligence President Bush used to justify our attacking Iraq was dead wrong. The intelligence that did not support the danger Bush and Cheney claimed existed from Iraq has been proven correct.

On February 10, 2006 the Washington Post carried the story of Paul R. Pillar, the retired CIA's top counterterrorism analyst from 2000 to 2005 who coordinated the intelligence on Iraq from 15 agencies. Pillar said Bush misused the intelligence and "cherry-picked" the intelligence to justify his decision to invade Iraq. The Washington Post story said Pillar wrote in an upcoming article for the Journal of Foreign Affairs that **"It has become clear that official intelligence was not relied on in making even the most significant national security decisions, which intelligence was misused publicly to justify decisions already made..."** These comments by Mr. Pillar are some of the most severe indictments of the way President Bush misused our intelligence to justify his invasion of Iraq in early 2003. Mr. Pillar said, "Official intelligence on Iraqi weapons programs was flawed, but even with its flaws, it was not what led to the war".

The consequences of this action are significant. Other countries not only expressed their opposition to the war but also have become wary of George Bush. Most of the countries view his leadership as bullish and brutish. Although the government of Great Britain supported Mr. Bush the British people did not support the war. Mr. Bush has not learned that in order to succeed against international terrorism and threats that exist, the United States must have the full and willing cooperation of the other nations in the world. We have received some cooperation; however it is not because of the atmosphere created by George Bush but because of the universal danger posed by terrorist attacks.

The Bush policy has isolated the U.S. from billions of people throughout the world. His credibility has been seriously impacted by the inability to locate any WMD in Iraq. After eight months of searching for these weapons, Mr. Kay believes that production was not resumed by Saddam Hussein after 1991. Colin Powell has now conceded that Iraq may not have had the weapons claimed by George Bush as the principal reason for the war. We must find a way to protect our nation in cooperation with the rest of the world. When we ignore world opinion we embark on a very dangerous path. Even General Powell has now stated that his speech before the U N on February 5, 2003 was the biggest mistake of his career.

The most dangerous reality is that millions of Muslims believe the policies of the United States and other Western countries threaten their belief, their territory and their God. Michael Scheuer, in his book Imperial Hubris states that America is faced with what he calls a *defensive jihad*, which is triggered by our policy in the Middle East. He points out that for Muslims do not separate politics and religion from their lives. They are all intertwined. For a Muslim to not join to protect Islam means that they are disobeying God's law. According to Mr. Scheuer the relationship of the Muslims to their religious beliefs is something that the Western world does not fully comprehend. Millions of Muslims look at Osama bin Laden as the protector of the Muslim faith, their way of life, their God and is not a terrorist. In fact the way Mr. Scheuer describes the conflict is more than just terrorism, it is an international insurrection by Muslims against what they believe is an attack on them, their religion and their way of life. The former CIA agent claims that we are faced with international insurrection by millions and millions of Muslims and that they will not end their resistance until the United States and other Western countries stop interfering with what they believe and remove themselves and their influence from all Muslim countries.

If this former CIA agent is correct, we have grossly understated the danger and the difficulty in dealing with what President Bush terms, "terrorism". It would do us well to look at the experience that Michael

Scheuer brings to the defense of our country and the western world. He believes that our invasion of Iraq has done more to energize the Islamic militants and thus weaken our security.

Social Security

For most Americans the issue of how to preserve Social Security is an important one. Publicly Bush supports the Social Security system and has acknowledged that the long-term prospect requires change. He understands that Social Security, as we know it, will be unable to meet its obligations within the next 40 years. To evaluate the Bush policy on Social Security it is helpful to understand some of the basics about the Social Security system.

The simple fact is that Social Security, from its inception, was an unfunded pension plan. It was created in the wake of the great Depression, which wiped out the assets of a generation of Americans. It was created to provide a minimal amount of retirement income to millions of American workers who had lost their life's savings and had no viable means of providing for their retirement years. The system was designed when people were expected to live only a few years past retirement and it was not designed to pay benefits to disabled workers. For the most part the system paid current benefits from current taxes. It was understood at times there would be some excess funds in the Social Security Trust Fund but it was not designed to hold the tax and pay it upon retirement.

When Social Security was enacted the demographics of this country were very different than they are today. In 1935 there were many working people paying into the system for every person receiving pension benefits. Therefore the issue of having enough money to pay benefits was not a problem. Some people still believe the money they had paid into Social Security is sitting someplace in a vault. Such is not the case and the money they paid into the system, for all practical purposes, has been paid out in benefits to people who have retired.

Some people believe the reason Social Security is in trouble is that the government misspent the money. That is not correct. The money was paid as envisioned to retirees, however, when you compare the amount of money paid into the system and the amount received from the system there is a significant imbalance. The first two generations who received Social Security benefits received as much as **20 times** more in benefits than the taxes they and their employer paid into the system. The system was designed when people were expected to live about five years after retirement. Today people are living 15 to 25 years beyond retirement and drawing benefits for three to five times longer than anticipated when the system was created.

Finally, the changing demographics have placed the last nail in the coffin. When the system was started 25 to 30 people were working and paying in to the system for each person receiving benefits. As the baby boomers retire, we will have two to three people paying in to the system for every person receiving benefits and the projections worsen. It does not take a major in mathematics to understand why Social Security is in trouble.

Clearly the president understood there was a need to do something and that is why he created the Presidential Commission on Social Security. He started with the answer, which for him, was to privatize Social Security. Therefore the Presidential Commission did not begin with a clean slate to view all possible solutions, but rather started with Mr. Bush's answer and worked back to the question. In addition Mr. Bush was careful to appoint members to the commission who shared his view of a solution. The results were three recommendations to partially privatize Social Security. In all three of the suggested solutions, monies would be diverted from younger workers Social Security taxes to create individual retirement accounts. The idea was to create a partially funded pension plan with the accumulation of the taxes diverted into the individual accounts plus the earnings produced by this money. It also provided for the transfer of this wealth between generations by allowing any unused amount in the individual accounts to pass at death.

Although this concept certainly has some positive facets, the basic question of how to pay benefits to the older workers while allowing younger workers to divert part of their Social Security taxes into the individual accounts was not addressed. It has been estimated a transition fund of over $4 Trillion would be needed to pay out expected benefits to the older retirees over the next 70 years. President Bush, nor the commission he appointed, identified a source to pay for this transition fund. It is not possible to implement such a policy without providing the funding to change from the current system to the proposed one.

Some suggested the use of General Fund revenue to transition the Social Security system. The reality of this suggestion ignores the national debt which will be at least $9 trillion by the end of the Bush second term without the added cost of Social Security and the $425 billion annual deficit that Bush plans to reduce to $260 Billion by 2009. That explosion in the national debt will cause the interest to skyrocket using up the money required for Social Security, Medicare, defense, education and most other needs of our country. Therefore President Bush supports a solution with no way of paying for his new system. This is one of the reasons why the former Secretary of the Treasury opposed the Bush tax cuts. He understood that there were significant needs to be met such as paying for Social Security. Unfortunately, when Mr. O'Neill explained that the tax cuts would eliminate the money required for things such as Social Security, the President, at the behest of his conservative cohorts, fired him. Had the President not hamstrung the commission and followed the advice of his Secretary of the Treasury, he may have been able to develop a viable solution to resolve the basic question of how to ensure the solvency of Social Security.

President Bush continues his discussions across the country about his change to Social Security. The Social Security question has two basic components. First, is the philosophy of what Social Security is and what it should be for workers in America? Second, is the mechanics of how to maintain the solvency of Social Security?

Social Security has always been a guaranteed minimum retirement benefit for the American worker. Something that was predictable and guaranteed. The problem with the Bush solution is that it alters the basic philosophy of Social Security. What George W. Bush is proposing is to convert the floor into an elevator. There is no question that individual equity accounts hold the potential of increasing a worker's retirement but it also holds the possibility of having less should the market be down at the time of a worker's retirement. There is a place for individual equity accounts and that place is over and above the minimum guaranteed floor of Social Security. Therefore, we should maintain the philosophy of Social Security as a guaranteed minimum and encourage workers to create individual equity accounts during their working life IN ADDITION to Social Security.

If we are to maintain a guaranteed minimum for Social Security, we need to fund the system through the bubble of the baby boomers. At the present time, 3 1/2 people are working for every one receiving benefits. At the present time, the taxes being collected are more than the benefits being paid out. Because of the baby boomers that will change starting in about 2018 and there will be only two people working for each person receiving benefits. When the baby boomer bubble has passed (in about 70 years), the system will right itself and return to a relationship similar to what exists today. Therefore, the issue is to finance retirement benefits under Social Security for the huge increase in population that occurred after World War II. That should be done by increasing the Social Security Trust Fund so it can bridge the funding deficit created by that bubble.

There are two suggestions that have been made to help fund the Social Security deficit. One is to augment the trust fund by General fund revenues which will require us to first balance the budget. The second idea is to extend the income limit on Social Security wages (currently the first $90,000 of earned income) the same as the Medicare tax. That would cause many billions of additional tax dollars to flow into the Social Security Trust Fund. That additional money could then be invested in equities to augment the yield to the trust fund over and above the 3% that the treasury bonds are currently paying on bonds held by the trust fund. This concept has been successfully used in EVERY state pension plan in the United States. Why would we not duplicate a successful strategy that is keeping our state pension plans solvent for Social Security?

The American people have contacted their Senators and Congressman to tell them that they want to maintain the minimum guaranteed Social Security system and have it funded by increasing the Social Security tax limit and investing that additional money in a sound mix of equity investments. Although some might benefit from the equity accounts proposed by President Bush, I believe the guaranteed Social Security income is far more important to the vast majority of Americans! The American people have spoken and they have rejected the Bush suggestion to partially privatize Social Security.

Medicare and Medicaid

President Bush appears to acknowledge that Medicare is in financial distress. He continually mentions modernizing Medicare but he is yet to offer any real solutions to both ensure coverage to seniors and find a way to pay for the coverage. Many of the same issues that are plaguing Social Security are also impacting Medicare. Changes in demographics and the fact people are living longer are major components adding to the costs to maintain the health of our seniors. In addition, Medicare has some elements that, in many respects, make the funding problem even more complex to solve.

The Bush administration has made several attempts to force seniors into a system employing the private sector. So far Congress has refused to force seniors into that situation. The new prescription drug benefit under Medicare has put this nose of the camel under the tent by limited test markets in which the private sector will be enlisted to provide medical care rather then the traditional Medicare system. Attempts to utilize HMO's have also not met with success either from a costs standpoint or from the acceptance of the seniors.

Some of the other issues that make the Medicare solution even more complicated are the fact that costs for healthcare rise a lot faster than inflation. The Cost of Living Adjustment (COLA) under Social Security only allows benefits to increase as much as inflation. Healthcare costs on the other hand have been raising many times the rate of inflation. Attempts by Medicare and the Bush administration to keep cost under control by limiting reimbursements are meeting with heavy resistance especially from doctors. For the first time, many physicians are considering to refuse Medicare because reimbursements are not keeping up with their added costs. If this happens it creates an immediate problem for seniors. If your physician were to opt out of Medicare, the senior would be responsible for the bill at the time of service. In addition they would most likely receive only a fraction of what the doctor charged for the service from Medicare. This eventuality will create a battleground between seniors and their physicians.

The in January 2005, Senator Kennedy asserted that 35% of every dollar spent by Medicare is for non-medical expenses. If this is correct, the first change should be to utilize technology and streamline procedures to reduce this 35% overhead to something more in the 10% range. This would mean an additional 25% of the Medicare expenditures would be used to meet the needs of our senior citizens. No company will allow one third of their costs to be incurred for overhead and neither should we tolerate this for Medicare.

A second issue that the Bush administration needs to answer is why is he focusing on Social Security and ignoring Medicare? The reality is that the size of the problem and the urgency of the funding shortfall in Medicare is far more serious than for Social Security. In March 2005, the Social Security and Medicare Trustees updated the condition of both systems. Their projections indicate that the Medicare Trust fund will be depleted in 2020 and Medicare will be able to pay 79% of claims after 2020. The Social Security Trust Fund will be depleted in 2041 and will be able to pay 73% of benefits after 2041. In addition the Social Security Trust fund is approaching $2 trillion while the Medicare trust fund is approximately one half of the trillion dollars. The health care issue is further complicated by the fact that 46 million Americans younger than 65 have no health insurance including 11 million children.

Why would anyone focus on the smaller problem while ignoring the larger one? Bush is worried about being struck by a bicycle while freight train is about to hit him!

The prescription drug legislation that President Bush supported will further exacerbate the funding problems for Medicare. The estimated cost during the first 10 years is in the neighborhood of $550 billion. There has been no funding source identified by the President or Congress to pay for this new medical benefit. The second 10-year projection cost for the new prescription drug benefit has ranged as high as $1 Trillion. In addition to the unfunded mandate created by the Bush Prescription plan are provisions that prevent seniors from purchasing prescription drugs outside the United States at lower costs or the purchase of insurance coverage to help pay the drug costs not covered under the new plan. In addition, President Bush has not provided any help to control the rapidly increasing cost of prescription drugs, which means both seniors and the tax payers will have to pay the higher costs. The real benefactors of the prescription drug plan crafted by the conservatives are the drug companies and the big losers will be seniors and the American Taxpayer. As of November 2005, neither Bush nor Congress has come up with one cent to pay for one of the largest increases in an entitlement program in our history.

Medicare taxes apply to all earned income unlike Social Security which is a cut off after the first $90,000 per year. That means the option to extend the tax to higher income wage earners has already been taken. Therefore to increase Medicare tax revenue would require an increase in the rate which would affect low and middle income wage earners the most. Another potential source to help fund the ever-increasing Medicare costs is the general fund. Here again the Federal deficit and higher interest created by the growing national debt make it doubtful that any significant help can be expected from General Fund revenue to help offset the increasing Medicare expense.

A specific ailment that has received some attention by the Bush administration is Alzheimer's disease. He has been supportive of research to help treat this disease. The impact of Alzheimer's disease given the impending retirement of the baby boomers could be catastrophic on both seniors and the Federal budget. Normally Medicare does not cover nursing home costs to treat Alzheimer's disease patients. However, if enough seniors run out of money and become eligible for Medicaid, the cost to care for Alzheimer's disease patients will become another Federal and State burden.

President Bush continues to express his intent to modernize Medicare, what ever that means. To date he has failed to produce any workable plan to pay the ever increasing cost of the health care needed by our seniors. In fact, with the passage of the prescription drug benefit he has moved us further away from a solution. It may be time for President Bush to create a presidential commission to take a look at the options to pay for Medicare. Hopefully, he will not make the same mistake he made with the Social Security Commission and appoint people who are not only knowledgeable but are able to consider all the possible ways to pay the increasing cost of health care for our seniors. The bottom line from the Bush policy on Medicare is the same as for Social Security: no help for seniors or the American Taxpayer

Medicaid is in even worse shape then Medicare. This health plan for the poor is jointly funded buy the Federal and state governments. The Bush solution to the growing cost in the Federal budget is to cut the Federal contribution and pass more of the cost to the states. The governors have told Bush they can not afford to make up the Federal cuts. States are looking for ways to cuts the cost during at time when more and more poor Americans need healthcare. Just after President Bush spoke in New Orleans about how Katrina has shed light on the plight of the poor, he and his supporters in Congress are cutting food stamps and Medicaid funding. There is not a single proposal to help 400,000 people replace their homes other then low interest loans that many will be unable to repay. The municipal governments have been forced to lay off their staff because their tax base has been destroyed and there is no funding for such things as police and fire. The Corps of Engineers only has funding to restore the levies around New Orleans to category 3 storms. We can however give Iraq, a country with the second largest oil reserves, a $ 20 billion dollar gift to rebuild parts of their country and spend almost $6 billion per month to fight a war that has not made us safer nor was justified in the first place. Weather it is Medicare, Medicaid or help for Americans that lost everything, the answer is the same, the federal Government has no money for the needs of the low or middle income Americans. We some how can find the money to cut taxes for the wealthy that do not need anything or tax cuts to oil companies that are making obscene profits or to help rebuild other countries.

Energy Policy

The energy policy of Mr. Bush, or lack of one, is an excellent example of how he approaches our national needs. Since 1973, it has been clear that the United States needed to become more independent from fossil fuel and the influence of the Middle East. The failure of the United States to develop a comprehensive policy to provide for our energy needs is not a new problem. Let's take a look at what our former oilmen have done to help resolve our energy needs.

Early in the administration of George Bush it was clear that he intended to take some action with respect to our energy needs. It is not surprising that he selected his vice president to head the task force that would produce the energy policy recommendation to Congress. The vice president, under his usual veil of secrecy, formed a task force and began consulting with a number of individuals in order to develop a plan that would eventually result in a legislative proposal.

From the outset, the White House treated this process like the Manhattan Project; everything went into Cheney's office, but nothing came out. Members of Congress, environmental groups and the press attempted in vain to learn more about what was going on during the development of the energy plan in vain. One of the most sought-after pieces of information was a list of the individuals that Mr. Cheney was consulting as part of his energy task force.

The vice president and the White House stonewalled the release of these names. They claimed, Executive Privilege. It is difficult to understand why the public was not entitled to know who the vice president was working with to develop something as important as the energy policy for the United States. Gradually rumors began to abound that most members of the task force were former top energy company executives, including the former Enron chairman, Ken Lay. Eventually, a lawsuit was filed in an attempt to force the vice president to release the names of the people he was consulting. In 2003, the federal appeals court ruled that the White House had to make public the names of the people who served on the energy task force. In September of 2003, President Bush directed an appeal be filed with the United States Supreme Court to overturn the lower court ruling. Two months after the administration asked the justices to review the case, Vice President Cheney and his longtime friend, Supreme Court Justice Scalia, had dinner at a restaurant on Maryland's Eastern shore. In January 2004, just after the court agreed to hear this case, Mr. Cheney went duck hunting in Louisiana with Justice Scalia.

This prompted many questions concerning the potential of a conflict of interest by the socializing with a member of the Supreme Court who was about hear the case. Charles Lewis, Director of the Center for Public Integrity, is quoted as saying, "It gives the appearance of a tainted process where decisions are not made on their merits when you have judges fraternizing with people before the court". David Bookbinder, the legal director of the Sierra Club, said, "It certainly raises a question about the appearance of impropriety, which is the standard that judges are held to".

Justice Scalia responded that there is no reason to question his ability to judge the case fairly. Numerous groups believe Scalia and Cheney should have kept their distance to avoid any possible appearance of conflict. Rogan Kersh, a Syracuse University political science professor said Scalia should withdraw from this case. In the end, the Supreme Court allowed Bush to keep the names secret but that does not answer the question of why should these names be keep from the American Public.

The most likely reason that President Bush and Vice President Cheney went to such lengths to keep the names of the people who served on the energy task force private appears to be in the legislation that resulted from the work of the task force.

The proposal that emerged is a taxpayer-funded giveaway to large mature energy companies. It appears the energy company executives helped themselves. The energy bill contained a plethora of issues that Bush wanted to push through Congress. The shortcomings of his energy policy are so numerous that it is hard to know where to begin.

First, the overall cost of his proposal is just short of $50 Billion. Second, the vast majority of the money goes to large energy firms to offset their exploration costs that they would realize even without the federal funds. The reason these companies would have conducted this exploration is that without it, they cannot continue to maintain their profits. This huge proposed Federal expenditure does not increase our energy supply it merely improves the profit picture for the large energy companies who would receive this money.

The energy legislation also contains the regulatory changes to enable the country to upgrade the electric grid. It contains permission to drill in Alaska, which has been rejected for years. The bill provides increased access to Federal lands to further help the large energy producers find gas and oil. There are some provisions to develop alternate fuels, build a gas pipeline in Alaska, develop the use of clean coal and help build new nuclear plants. The bill also provides help for such things as hydrogen co-generation projects and a host of miscellaneous items.

Bottom line the Bush energy plan was a $50 billion Christmas tree that would produce very little new energy at a time when we are running a $420 billion deficit. The bill is not doing enough to develop alternate energy sources that would be under the control of the United States, and it does nothing to require increased efficiency of cars and SUVs.

For too long we have looked only at the supply side of the energy equation. The real solution to make the United States more energy independent is to increase the efficiency of our cars, SUVs and trucks. Approximately half of the oil is consumed in the internal combustion engine. An increase of one-mile per gallon would save more oil than could be found in the Alaskan wilderness. Rather than include both incentives and penalties to help increase the efficiency of our motor vehicles, the Bush policy favors the supply side. It seems that conservatives are fixated with supply. They insist it is the solution to our energy needs as well as the solution to our economic growth.

The Energy Bill that finally became law in 2005 grants big oil over $12 billion in new tax cuts at a time when oil companies have posted huge profit increases. **Why would we add to the national debt with tax cuts to oil companies when they are making record breaking profits?**

Finally, the attitude of President Bush comes across in his energy policy. He refused to consider separating portions of the bill so that things like the electric grid and clean coal could move forward. He would not make the question of drilling in Alaska a separate bill. It is the same old approach: **my way or nothing**. The result is that in 2004, 31 years after our worst energy crisis we have no viable plan to move us forward with energy independence. We have no energy policy in place because the president is more interested in getting his way than meeting the needs of the nation. This is the same attitude he has toward our foreign policy, military policy and his solution to Social Security and Medicare funding. Why can't the president compromise in order to meet the needs of our nation?

It appears that Mr. Bush believes that **compromise means for him to listen and then do it his way.** This comes across time after time in the book, The Price of Loyalty by Ron Suskind.

Homeland Defense

President Bush deserves credit for the way he initially reacted to the 9/11 tragedy. His creation of the Department of Homeland Defense to bring together the various federal agencies was an essential component to deal with the security issue raised on that horrible day. He acknowledged it will take the cooperation of other nations in order to deal with these terrorist organizations and Mr. Bush sought international cooperation in areas such as intelligence, finance and law enforcement.

By the spring of 2003, the Bush administration had alienated most nations in the world with his insistence to attack Iraq. On one hand he was asking world leaders to help in the fight against terrorism while on the other hand telling them he did not need them when it came to Iraq. Although the United States is receiving more cooperation in its fight against international terrorism, the Bush attitude is not conducive to maximizing the cooperation we need from the other countries in the world.

Providing homeland defense is proving to be a very expensive undertaking. In some cases, federal agencies have their priorities altered while in other cases an increase in the funding is required. In fiscal year 2003 the homeland defense, including the amounts provided for border control and for Air Force Cover flights, amounted to about $38 billion. Although this is a sizable amount of money, many elements of our homeland defense are under funded. In addition, the cost to state and local governments continues to increase with little help from Washington.

Each time the federal government increases the alert status as it did before Christmas 2003, an additional $1.2 billion per week is required to defend the United States. State and local governments incur most of the cost. Washington is not helping the states and local governments to offset this huge increase in their expense. The type of alert system that has been developed applies to the whole country even if the threats are more localized. Refining the alert system to make it more area or threat specific would protect the country and reduce the financial impact.

In fiscal year 2003, local and state officials peppered the Bush administration and Congress for help that included: $6 billion for the states, $2.6 billion for cities and $3.5 billion for all other municipalities. President Bush only requested a portion of this funding from Congress. This failure will surely cause local taxes to rise that will negate the positive effects of his tax cuts.

Over three years after 9/11, there are glaring holes in our security. Port security remains almost non-existent with less than 5% of all shipping containers being inspected. We do not know what is in many cargo planes, small airports are totally unsecured and our borders are porous to say the least. The TV program 60 MINUTES aired a segment that showed people crossing into the United States from our southern border carrying things on their backs. When The INS was asked what these individuals were bringing in to the United States their answer was they did not have the manpower to confront these individuals. We only have cameras taking pictures.

The issue of equipment to first defenders is another area where President Bush has failed to provide the necessary money to buy the equipment needed. Funding for systems to protect civilian airliners from attack by shoulder-fired weapons such as the Stinger missiles has been discussed but there is no action to protect our airlines from attack. Funding to help state and municipal governments to defend against bio-terrorism is in short supply. The states are experiencing a $40 to $50 billion-dollar deficit and the federal budget is not providing the help required. Governors and mayors have repeatedly told the Bush administration they need additional funding. Although President Bush has been requesting additional funding for Homeland

Defense, there are many under-funded elements that still have not been addressed.

It is hard to assess the consequences of our incomplete response to fund Homeland Defense. It is hard to believe the Congress would not approve the money if the President requested it. Should a terrorist group successfully use WMD against the United States because of these holes in our defense; the Bush administration will be hard-pressed to explain their inactions. Porous borders, unsecured ports, un-inspected cargo planes and unsecured small airports are some more glaring areas where Homeland Defense is inadequate or nonexistent. At a time when we have such urgent Homeland Defense requirements, we see our president sending money to rebuild Iraq, and proposing to make his tax cuts permanent. A study by the Brookings Institute recently estimated that making the 2001, 2002 and 2003 tax cuts permanent, as President Bush requested, would increase the federal deficits through 2014 by an additional $2 trillion.

President Bush continues not to provide border security. He admitted we are short 10,000 border guards while at the same time only requested added funding for 200 additional border guards. WHY? Border States are being forced to take action to stem the influx of illegal aliens while Bush wants to grant legal status to millions of people that have broken our laws. Bush does not enforce existing laws that are intended to punish companies that hire illegal aliens. WHY?

Homeland Defense is yet another example of how we are burying our heads in the sand. Our spending is increasing at a rapid rate, we need additional funding in so many areas and President Bush wants to further cut the resources available to pay our bills. This is an example of the **"charge and spend"** policy of President Bush.

Education - Almost no child left behind under President Bush

President Bush, the education president, as late as his State of The Union Address in 2004, touts his No Child Left Behind Act. This is the federal law George Bush pushed through Congress to improve education. It is based on the "Texas miracle" in Houston with the claim that their dropout rates plunged and test scores soared.

Bush praised the Houston school Superintendent Rod Paige, who was given credit for this miracle cure for poor education. When George Bush became president of the United States he immediately nominated Mr. Paige for secretary of education.

As reported by Dan Rather, the accounts of some of the miracles in Houston are untrue. "I was shocked. How can this be", said Robert Kimball an assistant principal at the Sharpston High School. The claim was that **not a single student had dropped out at his school during 2001-2002. In fact, 463 students dropped out of Sharpston High School during that year.** There is quite a difference from zero dropouts to 463 dropouts. The Texas miracle claimed a drop out rate district wide of 1.5%. A 60 MINUTES II audit found that there was a small error and that the actual dropout rate appears to be as high as **50%** in the Houston school district in 2001-2002.

Yes, someone "cooked the books." This would be bad enough if it were just the Houston school district but now we have a new law, the centerpiece of the Bush education policy, designed after a plan that is a fraud. We also have a Secretary of Education who was credited with this plan by none other then President George W. Bush.

When the Houston school district officials were confronted by 60 MINUTES II, they would not talk on camera. The claim of the Houston school district officials was that the audit performed by 60 MINUTES II only proved "outright fraud" at the Sharpston High

School. The false statistic at the other Houston schools was blamed on "confusion" about the complex state coding system.

Bottom-line, the Bush "No Child Left Behind" law is based on a lie. What was the reaction of our Secretary of Education, Mr. Paige? He declined to answer 60 MINUTES II. How did President Bush react? He has totally ignored these revelations and is pushing ahead with his "miracle plan" for improving education as if the miracle were true. What a sad commentary for something as important as public education. There may be some things that the Houston school district is doing well, but the lies about their drop-out rate casts a long shadow over their plan to improve public education.

Finally, when we look at the funding of public education some believe that the federal government provides a significant amount of the resources to educate our children. Nothing could be further from the truth; over 95% of the money spent on public education comes from state and local taxes and almost all of the educational requirements are approved by local and state action. That's not to say that the federal government does not help especially with remedial training in math and reading. However, the real key to successful education lies at the local and state level. That is why this fraud and deception by the Houston public school system is so disappointing. The Houston School district is the local level and if we have corruption and outright misinformation at the bottom it is difficult to understand how we can move forward and provide the kind of education necessary to ensure future generations will be able to compete in the world of tomorrow. The capstone to the Bush education policy failure is that he under funded his own plan by $24 Billion dollars through FY 2005.

Foreign Policy

The changes in foreign policy under the Bush administration will have a long-term impact on both the United States and other countries. There is little doubt; the changes in our foreign policy under George W. Bush have been significant. In Ron Suskind's book, The Price of Loyalty, President-elect Bush was quoted regarding his election mandate by saying, "We must heal, whatever wounds may exist". Mr. Bush went on to say, "At times there would be disagreement and that's OK. If this were a dictatorship it would be a heck of a lot easier, just so long as I am the dictator".

In the very first speech given by Mr. Bush after the Supreme Court settled the 2000 election, he said, "I want to be the president of all Americans". This gave many who were unhappy with the election results some hope. It was certainly true that George Bush was not given an electoral mandate to make radical changes.

At the same time Dick Cheney on the CBS program *Face the Nation* made it clear that "the agenda of President-elect Bush was carefully developed and he had **no intention at all on backing off it"**. It quickly became clear; George Bush had a style more like that of a dictator than a person that would bring consensus. He has a disarming way of listening and then moving on with his own predetermined course of action. The result was just like Dick Cheney explained on <u>FACE THE NATION</u>. Mr. Bush was not to be deterred from moving with the radical changes of his agenda. The fact that Mr. Bush received 500,000 fewer votes than Al Gore made no difference. The fact that he was elected because 3,500 votes were thrown out in Palm Beach County, Florida due to a poorly designed ballot made no difference. The uncompleted recount of the votes in Florida (including 27,000 in Duval County) made no difference. It was to be the "Bush Way" at home and abroad.

From the outset our foreign policy was not the diplomatic approach of Colin Powell but rather the, "do it my way" style of George W. Bush. It's a miracle that Colin Powell lasted given the differences in style between him and Bush, Cheney, Rumsfeld and Rove. Eventually however Powell caved in to using our military power against Iraq. His speech on February 5, 2003 clearly signaled that he had given in to Bush et al.

Some of the most important changes in our foreign policy since January 20, 2001 include our approach to the Middle East conflict, the way we are dealing with North Korea as well as the preemptive use of our military against Iraq. All these changes however were produced by the same Bush style that has created distrust and dislike toward President Bush. The approach of Mr. Bush is not to move toward the middle ground when there is a difference of opinion. The Bush style is, it must be my way. This has produced some of the strongest differences at home between conservatives and almost everyone else in this country just like the rift with our allies such as Germany and France. Also the people of Great Britain did not agree with Mr. Bush even though he was able to gain the support of the British Prime Minister.

Mr. Bush employs the same combative and swaggering approach to most everything. It does not matter if it is the missile defense system, the environment, North Korea, the Middle East conflict, economic and tax policy, immigration, Social Security, or health care. The conservatives defend the Bush style as that of a strong leader. That does not apply to Mr. Bush because a leader is one who will get people to go to a place they would not otherwise go. Mr. Bush was unable to lead the vast majority of other countries into Iraq or to help restore order after the war.

Where are these radical shifts in policy coming from? It is doubtful that George W. Bush, given his very limited experience and knowledge of foreign affairs, has developed his policies by himself. One theory is that the Republican leadership chose Mr. Bush because they knew he could be molded into doing what they wanted. Key players such as Cheney, Rove, Rumsfeld, and unnamed corporate executives have packed his head with what they wanted. When you take a look at the background of Mr. Bush prior to becoming president, you'll find someone who did not have a lot of major successes. He was not a very successful businessman in Texas. He did make some money when he owned the Texas Rangers and that came about because of his contacts.

The military service of George W. Bush is another sordid issue. To evaluate his service in the Texas Air National Guard we need to concentrate on three areas. First, what was his motivation to join the guard? Second, did he receive preferential treatment getting into the guard as well as his early release with an honorable discharge? Finally, did he fulfill his responsibilities while a member of the Texas Air National Guard?

As to the first issue, George W. Bush's application clearly stated that "he did not want to be sent overseas", (Vietnam). The reality was that during Vietnam, service in the National Guard was a sure way not to be sent to war.

How George W. Bush got into the guard has been established by the former Speaker of the Texas House of Representatives who acknowledged that he got George W. Bush into the guard ahead of many other applicants. At the time Mr. Bush applied to the guard, there was a one year waiting period and over 100 applicants ahead of him. In addition, his former professor at Harvard stated that George W. Bush told him that he got into the guard through the influence of family contacts and also received an early honorable discharge via their efforts.

Finally, he failed to take a required annual physical that resulted in him being grounded as a pilot. That is documented from his military records in the order that grounded him. The reason George W. Bush was granted a position in the Texas Air National Guard was to be a pilot. Therefore, his refusal to obey the regulations to get the physical meant that he did not fulfill the obligations he accepted when commissioned in the guard. His refusal to take the required physical was confirmed by the former secretary of his commanding officer. In addition, during the second half of 1972, George W. Bush did not attend required drills for a period of six months and is documented by his military pay records as well as his Officer Efficiency Report.

To summarize George W. Bush's military service one would have to come to the conclusion that he joined the guard to avoid service in Vietnam. He got into the guard and was granted an early honorable discharge because of preferential treatment. He did not fully meet his obligations to the guard and avoided the consequences because of preferential treatment. If that is the standard of honorable service to our country, I believe we need a much higher standard!

Any accomplishments as Governor of Texas are more the result of the Legislature, since it's the Legislature, and not the Governor that has the real power in Texas. When Mr. Bush was first elected there was much speculation that the staff had much more experience than the president. The voters did not elect the president's staff they elected the president to run the nation.

Mr. Bush constantly chides the congress when it fails to pass his legislative initiatives. He has forgotten that it is Congress who makes the laws. It is Congress who passes the budget. It is Congress who declares war. The attitude of the president and his staff is that Congress has the responsibility to support the proposals of the president. Congress is to be a big rubber stamp and when they do not agree with Mr. Bush they are disloyal to the Commander-in-Chief. Mr. Bush does not seem to realize his principal responsibility is to enforce the laws passed by Congress. He is expected to provide suggestions that may be accepted or not accepted by the legislative branch of our government. How often have you heard Mr. Bush say he is taking an issue directly to the people when he fails to get his way? I guess he gets back to his initial statement after election about it being easier, "if it were a dictatorship."

The most significant foreign policy change that has taken place under President Bush is our preemptive use of our vast military power. In modern times, this is the first time the United States used its military the way President Bush did in Iraq. We are told by the President and Vice President that we must be prepared to use our military in preemptive fashion to prevent terrorists from attacking our people. There is no question if the United States is in danger of being attacked it is the responsibility of the President to do everything within his power to defend the United States. Recall the Cheney speech when he said we could not wait for the smoking gun in Iraq because it might be a mushroom cloud over one of our cities. President Bush, Dick

Cheney, Secretary Rumsfeld and later Colin Powell all insisted we were at immediate risk from Saddam Hussein. Today we know that was not the case. Now the reason for the war was to free the people of Iraq and enforce the UN resolutions. All the rhetoric about Iraq having weapons of mass destruction and being in a position that would truly threaten the United States is simply not true. **It is not acceptable to place our military in jeopardy to remove evil dictators or to enforce UN resolutions. The only acceptable reason to risk the lives of our military is to protect this country.**

Mr. Bush used or manipulated the intelligence information to help convince Congress, the American people and the United Nations that we were in danger from Iraq. Either our intelligence was in error or the facts were distorted to justify the war in Iraq. It also appears that the decision to remove Saddam Hussein was made long before 9/11. The policy of President Bush has diverted the resources needed to confront the real danger to our country, which is from international terrorism. Thus, we have not resolved our security problem and have created yet another terrorist operation called Iraq. Even if we are able to create a democratic government in Iraq, al-Qaeda and other terrorists groups who pose the real danger to the United States are operating throughout the world. President Bush is convinced the establishment of a democracy in Iraq is what the people want and that it will spread through the region. Although the people of Iraq are glad to be rid of Saddam Hussein, there is no assurance they want a western style democracy. The Bush policy of the "spreading democracy" in the Middle-East may turn out to be a failure and then we have sacrificed over 2,100 American lives, 35,000 injured military members and hundreds of billions of dollars for what? The Bush policy in Iraq is to impose what he thinks is best for them. It will be interesting to see what type of government finally develops in Iraq.

Another very important Bush foreign policy was in the Middle East. At the beginning of his term, he had a hands off approach and insisted that the Israelis and Palestinians settle the dispute among themselves. When the violence began to spiral out of control, it became clear that this policy was not working and was dangerous. Allowing the conflict between Israel and Palestine to expand into other countries in the Middle-East was simply unacceptable.

At that point Mr. Bush became more engaged and developed his "Roadmap To Peace" plan which envisioned a separate Palestinian state alongside Israel. This plan received the support of our European allies, Russia and the Arab countries. It showed some real promise to bring peace to this part of the world. However, President Bush failed to insist that the terms of this plan were followed by both parties. He did not force the Palestinian Authority to disarm the radical groups that were attacking Israel. There was a period of 90 days when a cease-fire was put in place and the violence against Israel subsided. At the same time President Bush refused to force Israel to abide by its part of the Roadmap to Peace. His plan required Israel to give up settlements in the Palestinian territories and to withdraw its troops from that area. Instead Israel continued to build new settlements and made very little attempt to remove the illegal settlements they had built outside Israel. They continued their attacks in civilian areas against the leaders of Hamas and other terrorist groups causing continued civilian casualties which enraged the Palestinians. In addition, Israel began building a wall to protect itself that goes beyond the borders of Israel and unilaterally changes its borders at the expense of the Palestinians.

This policy of President Bush is viewed by the Palestinians as one-sided and results in aggravating anti- American sentiment throughout Moslem world.

Trade Policy

The trade policy of the Bush administration is for the most part a continuation of the free-trade movement that began years ago. There are however changes taking place that will require a more comprehensive approach to free-trade. The most recent trend is a thing called "off shoring". This is the outsourcing of white-collar jobs by American companies to China and India to lower their costs and increase their profits.

Paul Craig Roberts, a senior research fellow at the Hoover Institute, said that the loss of these white-collar jobs have undermined the principal of comparative advantage. If comparative advantage is the basis for free-trade, how can it exist when the factors of production are as mobile as the goods?"

Prior to this off shoring, the issue was competing with manufacturers in other countries where the production costs were less than in the United States. Today we see parts of the production process being contracted to overseas firms and the ultimate consequence of this action is unclear. In addition to the loss of American jobs, is the dissemination of information abroad. When you call customer service to ask a question about your insurance policy and you speak to someone in India, it raises the question of your personal information available halfway across the world.

Another very troubling issue is the illegal duplication of products and the total disregard for copyright and patent protection. Companies in China are illegally duplicating American cars. Although these cars have not appeared on our streets, they are preventing the sale of our vehicles in China since they sell for a fraction of the price of our product.

The government of China sets its own currency exchange rates artificially below market levels. The result of this is to make their products cheap relative to our products and ads to the trade deficit. The problem with the Bush trade policy is that it has not helped resolve these issues or create a level playing field for American companies and American workers. Every week the statistics document our job loss and the increase in the trade deficit. It takes more than lip service to ensure free trade. What we need is a trade policy that promotes free trade, protects American workers and provides a level playing field for us.

The Bush trip to China in November 2005 produced nothing to deal with the growing trade imbalance with China. The policy of Bush toward trade is expand a policy that has resulted in a record trade deficits and the loss of American Manufacturing jobs.

To illustrate the impact of or trade policy lets take a look at the clothing industry which is in danger of being eliminated in this country.

Some people indicate that when we buy cheaper clothing from China, the American consumer gets lower prices and Wal-Mart and their staff benefit. It is true that the profits and labor associated with retailing the cheaper clothing from China does help both Wal-Mart and its employees. The financial problems of GM and Ford are the next sector to be impacted and the most recent cuts by GM of 9% of its work force and the closing on 9 plants is a prime example.

What is lost are the company profits and all the jobs involved with producing the clothing which is a lot greater than the profit and labor from the retailing side. In the long-run, the benefit derived from the lower prices is more than offset by the loss in profits and jobs from the manufacture of clothing and textiles. Without living wage jobs, the American consumer will not have the money to purchase the lower priced imports in the future.

This is but one example we have seen. The very same thing happened in electronics and to a lesser degree in the automobile industry. If we expand this trade policy into Central America, our sugar industry will be in danger the same as our textile and clothing industries. Clearly the trade policies we have been following for the past 12 years has not produced a level playing field and has resulted in the loss of jobs as well as entire industries. That impacts both our economy and the strategic interests of this country.

Environment

The Bush policy on the environment is no surprise. He made it clear that he intended to relax environmental protection requirements to reduce the economic impact on business. The Green Party brought one irony of the 2000 election to us when they ran Ralph Nader for president. They placed protection of our environment at the top of their agenda. As it turned out, Ralph Nader gave George Bush the election since every vote for their candidate came from Vice President Al Gore who favored protecting the environment. It was more important for the Green party to make a statement and qualify for the Federal election funds than to protect the environment.

Across the entire spectrum, there has been a steady march away from environmental protection under George W. Bush. His appointment of Christie Whitman did appear to slow him down a bit, but she finally went the way of Paul O'Neill when it became clear she had a different opinion from Mr. Bush. Like everything else, extremes generally do not produce what is best for the majority of people. That is true politically and it is the case when protecting our environment. To set environmental protection requirements too high creates serious impediments to economic growth. One specific example is the extent some groups have gone to in Florida to protect the Manatee. If some people had their way there would be no more boats or use of the waterways. The economic impact of that extreme would destroy the economy in many parts of Florida. What is needed is a policy in the middle that does not abuse our environment while, at the same time, does not create rules and regulations that destroy the economy.

The list of changes made by President Bush to roll back environmental protection provisions is extensive. One of the more serious actions is the relaxation of corporate average fuel economy (CAFÉ) standards. This change effects both the environment and our ability to move closer to energy independence. This issue is covered in greater detail under the energy policy section of this book. President Bush has refused to abide by the regulations to control carbon dioxide as required by the Clean Air Act and returned snowmobiles to Yellowstone Park He pushed leasing Federal lands in Alaska and Florida and reduced air conditioning efficiency standards. In 2002, he was the only major world leader not to attend the World Summit on Sustainable Development. The Bush policy on the environment is clear: roll back most of the rules that were in place.

The most contentious part of his rollback is the greenhouse gas issue and global warming. At the center of this issue is the Kyoto treaty that President Bush refused to sign. The impact of global warming is probably one of the most difficult issues because the science is not clear as to what impact mankind can have on our climate. There's certainly evidence to show the earth has undergone cycles of warming and cooling throughout the eons of its history. Experts will continue to argue who is right and only time will be able to definitively answer this question. There is however little doubt that the environment will not be nearly as pristine or clean under George W. Bush as it would have been under a presidency of Al Gore.

Summary of the First Term

The objective of my book, <u>George W. Bush Robin Hood For the Rich.</u> is to provoke thought in the mind of the reader as to how the Bush policies have impacted his or her life. This is but one step in the process of becoming a more informed.

National policy should be in consort with the wishes of the majority and not reflect simply the desires of the extremes to either the right or the left. I personally believe that when the power is split between the Republicans and the Democrats there is a lot better chance that our overall policy will be more centrist and provide for the things that the majority of Americans desire. Governing from either the right or the left is not in the best long-term interest of the United States and is not best for our democracy.

Clearly the Bush administration's policies tend to be to the right and fail to address many of the important issues sought by either the moderate or the liberal voters in our country. The Bush administration clearly makes choices based on politics rather than what is best for the majority over the long-term. This can be seen most clearly in the economic and tax policies that President Bush has pushed through Congress.

The policy shift of George W. Bush that will most likely have the greatest impact on our lives is the growth in the national debt and the huge increase in the interest it will require. The Bush **charge and spend policy**, its tax cuts to the wealthy and the failure to create jobs that pay a living wage is the major cause for the huge increase in our national debt. The conservatives blame the deficit and the growing national debt on 9/11. It is certainly true we are spending far more to defend ourselves due to the events of that tragic day. However, the real shortfall of the Bush policy is that his economic policy failed to stimulate the economy to produce jobs and has not created the needed federal revenue to pay for these additional expenses. Rather, his tax cuts have been only marginally effective in producing a level of economic growth to replace the revenue lost from the tax cuts and pay for the increased costs to defend our country.

Another retort from the right is that the economic downturn began at the end of the Clinton administration. That is absolutely correct. What we are looking at is how effective have the Bush policies been to stimulate our economy and overcome the downturn. How effectively have his policies provided jobs? The Bush administration points to increases in the stock market, increases in productivity and higher corporate profits as proof that his policies are working. The only proof that makes any difference is the bottom line with respect to our ability to pay for the needs of our country. Is the economy growing at a rate that is producing the additional revenue to balance the budget? Are the tax cuts producing jobs for American workers? The answer to those questions is clearly a resounding no. We have a $400-500 billion annual deficit and we should have created 6 million jobs to keep up with the population growth since George Bush took office and have only created about 4.5 million new jobs. The Bureau of Labor Statistics has calculated that between January 2001 and January 2005, the Bush policies have produced a net increase of 119,000 jobs. That is just 5 million less than the new workers seeking jobs since January 2001! Where are the jobs for these 5 million American workers? Bush has the worst job creation record since President Herbert Hoover just before the great Depression. People without work do not benefit from higher corporate profits or from

53

increased productivity unless it creates a job for them. To make up for these 5 million jobs that were not created during the first term of President Bush, his policies need to produce 250,000 every month during the second term to provide for the growth during the second term and make up for the first term deficit. What makes a difference to workers is a job that enables them to live from day to day not stock market increases or corporate profit improvement. When you view the results of the last five years on the low and middle income Americans, the results from the Bush tax and economic policies are an abject failure.

The impact from using our military in a preemptive fashion will depend on how we employ them in the future. If we only use our great power to defend the United States when it is truly in danger, then the Iraq war will remain an isolated mistake. If however, we continue to use our military power preemptively to remove evil dictators or promote régime change, we will create instability and fear in the world.

The Bush policies on education, as poor as they are, will not have a major impact on how well we educate our children. The fact is that educational funding and control of public education rests at the local and state levels. The impact of the Federal government is marginal at best.

The long-term impact of the Bush backpedaling on the environment will add more days when the sun will be obscured and people with breathing disorders will have difficulty going outside. The larger question of global warming is not nearly so clear. Scientists on both sides of this issue can cite data that either supports or refutes the issue of whether or not anything mankind can do will in the long run change our climate. It is clear that major shifts in global temperature have occurred many times in the past.

The Bush policies on Social Security and Medicare are non-solutions to ensuring the solvency of those social programs. The real consequence of the Bush policies lie in the economic morass he has created. The fact that we have cut Federal taxes, increased the Federal deficit and the higher interest it will mandate, will mean we will have less resources to ensure the solvency of these two social programs.

The impact of the Bush attitude toward other countries is that we are going it alone in Iraq, which has added to American casualties and American costs. The only solution is for President Bush to change his approach.

The impact of President Bush ignoring the repair of our infrastructure will increase the cost when the repairs cannot be delayed. In addition, available revenue, given the tax cuts and the increased debt and interest will make it difficult to pay for these repairs.

The trade policy of Mr. Bush has continued the trade deficits we have seen from other administrations. On one hand we support free-trade but on the other hand we allow other countries to establish roadblocks to the importation of our goods. We allow them to create conditions that make it difficult for American countries to compete. Things such as allowing China to establish an artificial exchange rate that works against the sale of our goods in their country and make their goods cheaper to us are examples of problems the Bush trade policy has ignored. Duplicating American goods is another practice that is being followed by foreign countries, especially China. Free-trade to be truly free cannot create impossible competitive situations for American companies and result in the loss of jobs. Continued trade policies like the ones we are currently seeing will have a detrimental impact on our economy and job creation.

At this point, take a few moments to answer the following questions.
Since George W. Bush took office:

Are you and your family better off financially?
Have the tax cuts helped you?
Do you feel more secure?
Has the way other nations view America improved?
Have we begun rebuilding our infrastructure?

Can you afford healthcare and prescription drugs?
Are we doing enough for Homeland defense?
Have we made Social Security financially secure?
Have we made Medicare financially secure?
Have we created jobs?
Are we controlling our borders?
Are we repaying the national debt?
Is America more politically polarized?
Are we protecting the environment?
Has our trade deficit improved?

Section Two - Suggested policy changes.

Spending

Review discretionary non defense expenditures including "pork barrel" spending to cut our budget. Change legislative procedures to end tacking non related expenditures to bills and require all appropriations to go through the normal process. Any emergency appropriations should be dealt with as stand alone bills

Taxes

Restore the tax rates on the top two income tax brackets to the pre-2000 levels.

Restore tax rates on capital gains and dividends to pre- 2000 levels.

Make permanent the increased child credit, elimination of the marriage penalty, the 10% bracket and increase the level of income that triggers the alternate tax. That increased level should then be indexed to cost-of-living each year so that the threshold for the alternate tax remains constant after inflation.

Retain the federal estate tax with the following changes:

Provide a $2 million exemption per person and increase that exemption each year by the cost-of-living.

Provide deferment of any federal estate tax on family farms or family business so long as they pass to members of the immediate family – children, grandchildren or siblings. If the family business or farm is later sold to a non-family entity, the tax in the amount due at passing would be paid upon sale.

Close corporate loopholes that allow avoiding corporate income taxes by moving off shore. Provide surtax on companies that export American jobs to other countries and provide tax credits to companies who create or restore jobs from overseas to the United States. Insure corporations pay their fair share of taxes.

Consider new ways to help small businesses compete and to fund employee health insurance.

Simplify the progressive tax system by eliminating most of the existing loop holes in the tax code.

Deficit

Establish the objective to bring our general fund expenses and revenues into balance by 2008.

Begin generating a budget surplus of $200 billion annually starting with fiscal year 2009. This annual surplus would be directly applied each year to reduce the overall federal deficit.

Below is a process that should be considered to achieve the fiscal discipline outlined above namely to balance revenues and expenditures by 2008 and generate a fiscal surplus of $200 billion starting in 2009:

Evaluate tax incentives and or expenditures that would increase the growth rate (GDP) in an effort to generate more jobs and create additional federal revenue. Areas to consider should include tax incentives to stimulate such things as alternate energy sources and higher auto, SUV and truck gas mileage. Invest federal tax dollars to begin rebuilding the infrastructure of our country. These expenditures would be paid to private companies to complete the necessary reconstruction projects in order to create jobs and corporate profits.

If the added revenue from the increased GDP growth together with expenditure reductions does not achieve the overall objectives of balancing the budget and then creating a fiscal surplus, the tax structure needs to be examined for additional revenue sources. In no event, other than national emergency or declared war, should the United States spend more than it collects in revenue after 2008. In addition, we need to generate and apply the $200 Billion annual surplus to the repayment of the national debt until it is repaid, (approximately 30 years).

Failure to achieve this objective will have a devastating impact on our needs in the future. Issues such as additional funding for Social Security and Medicare, national defense, education and the rebuilding of our infrastructure make it essential that we end the practice of charging to the future the things that we need for our society.

Energy

Restore the Café standards and make them apply to all cars, trucks and SUVs.

Establish new targets for increased miles per gallon for each type of vehicle over the next 10 years.

Establish tax credits for car manufacturers who achieve the established standards.

Establish tax surcharges to car manufacturers who fail to meet the new mileage standards.

Utilize the additional tax revenue from surcharges to help fund the tax credits to corporations who achieve the new Café standards.

Provide federal subsidies to more fully utilize available coal supplies to create the energy needed wherever possible. Subsidies should be used to help provide for clean air equipment and to research new methods of utilizing coal in a non polluting way. Tax credits should also be used to convert existing oil and gas fired generators to coal and with the cost of transporting coal from the source to the user.

Provide subsidies to help car manufacturers develop cars and trucks using alternate propulsion systems such as fuel cells and hybrid/electric vehicles.

Provide subsidies to develop long-term renewable energy supplies including geothermal, wind, direct solar conversion, cold fusion, fuel cells etc. The objective would be to reduce our dependence on foreign oil as well as provide for the sale of the new technology and equipment to other countries. This would have the obvious advantage of not only solving our energy problem but eliminating many of the political entanglements that our dependence on Middle East oil creates. In addition, a reduction in the purchase of foreign oil would help our balance of trade as would selling the new technology and equipment to other countries. Thus this strategy would be a win-win-win-win situation for our countries by enhancing employment, corporate profits, reduce our trade deficit as well as simplifying some of our political entanglements.

Encourage the development of natural gas in areas controlled by the United States

Encourage the development of additional oil supplies that are under the control of the United States and do not endanger the environment.

Carefully evaluate any new or renewed agreements to provide United States produced energy to other nations. Our objective should be to first provide for energy independence before pledging our assets, especially oil and gas, to other countries.

Social Security

Stop any attempt to extend Social Security benefits to illegal aliens.

Continue the gradual increase of full retirement to age 70. Allow retirement as early as 62 with actuarial reduction in benefits.

Consider limiting the payout to retirees with non-Social Security income above $150,000 per year. When a retired couple has non-Social Security income above $150,000 per year (index this amount each year by cost of living), the benefit under Social Security would end at the point in which the individual's contribution had been completely returned to the taxpayer. For example, if an individual during their lifetime paid $70,000 in Social Security taxes, excluding their employer contribution, their Social Security payments would terminate if their non-Social Security income exceeded the maximum amount when they reach a total payout of $70,000 in this example.

Should a retiree's non-Social Security income fall below the maximum amount, the Social Security payments would resume based on their original entitlement so long as their non-Social Security income remained below the maximum amount.

Re-examine the option of allowing workers to set aside 2% or 4% of their Social Security tax to individual accounts. Issues to be evaluated should include:

Develop realistic estimates as to the transition costs. Identify the source needed to fund this transition amount before deciding to implement this change. **In no event should any portion of the transition funding be borrowed.**

Consider the impact on a worker who selects the private account option wherein the value of their account at the time of retirement was less than the total benefits that would be paid under the traditional Social Security amount. Would there be a provision to subsidize the payment of the amount received under the individual retirement option to bring it equal to the traditional Social Security benefit?

Evaluate an alternative to the individual equity account that would allow portions of the Social Security Trust Fund to be invested in stock market index funds. This would provide the advantage of increased earnings equity investments produce without the high cost to maintain millions of small accounts that would be required under the individual account concept. **This idea has been successfully used by every state pension fund in the United States as well as many large corporate pension plans.**

Consider lifting the income limit upon which Social Security taxes are paid to include **all earned income** similar to the current Medicare tax. This additional revenue would be used as the source for the transition funding required to convert the Social Security system to a partially privatized configuration or to solve the solvency issue by allowing an enlarged trust fund to be invested in equities.

Let's take a look at the Bush proposal for Social Security private accounts. Below is a table which shows the results of allowing workers to set aside $1000 in year one and increase that investment by $100 per year from their Social Security taxes. Although President Bush has indicated that 4% of a worker's Social Security taxes would be diverted to an individual account, his fine print limits the contribution to $1,000 in the first year and allows an increase of $100 each year thereafter. The column on the right shows the cumulative balance using an 8% compounded rate of return. As you can see, the amount of money that a worker would have at retirement under the Bush plan is NOT significant unless you participate for 35-40 years or more.

Thus, even if Bush can come up with the trillions of dollars to replace the amount transferred to the individual accounts plus the trillions of dollars to fully fund the benefits for older workers or people who do not select the individual accounts, only workers under the age of 30 would benefit in any way from this proposal. If we borrow the money required for Social Security, the interest on the trillions needed will eliminate any benefit even to the youngest worker:

Year	Annual Contribution Per the Bush plan	Cumulative balance before earnings	Cumulative balance with 8% compounded earnings
1	$ 1,000	$ 1,000	$ 1,080
2	1,100	2,180	2,354
3	1,200	3,554	3,838
4	1,300	5,138	5,549
5	1,400	6,949	7.504
6	1,500	9,004	9,724
7	1,600	12,924	13,958
8	1,700	15,658	16,910
9	1,800	18,710	20.206
10	1,900	22,106	23,875
11	2,000	25,875	27,945
12	2,100	30,034	32,449
13	2,200	34,649	37,420
14	2,300	39,720	42,898
15	2,400	45,298	48,922
16	2,500	51,422	55,536
17	2,600	58,136	62,786
18	2,700	65,486	70,725
19	2,800	73,525	79,408
20	2,900	82,307	88,892
21	3,000	91,892	99,243
22	3,100	102,343	110,531
23	3,200	113,731	122,830
24	3,300	126,129	136,220
25	3,400	139,620	150,789
26	3,500	154,289	166,632
27	3,600	170,232	183,850

28	3,700	187,550	202,554
29	3,800	206,355	222,863
30	3,900	226,763	244,904
31	4,000	248,904	268,816
32	4,100	272,916	294,750
33	4,200	298,950	322,866
34	4,300	327,166	353,339
35	4,400	357,739	386,358
36	4,500	390,858	422,127
37	4,600	426,727	460,865
38	4,700	465,565	502,810
39	4,800	507,610	548,219
40	4,900	553,119	597,368

If the yield of 8% net after expenses is not achieved, the reduction in the totals will be significant. This was calculated from the Bush plan outlined in www.gop.com.

Social Security Math

For a worker age of 53, their account value at age 68 would be $48,922 with an 8% compounded yield per year. Adjusted for inflation at 3% that is the equivalent of $30,980 today.

For a worker age 43 their account value at age 68 would be $150,789 with an 8% compounded yield. Adjusted for inflation at 3% that is the equivalent of $70,442 today.

For a worker age 28 their account value at age 68 would be $597,368 with an 8% compound yield. Adjusted for inflation at 3% that is the equivalent of $176,649 today.

The truth is that the Bush plan mathematically does not work unless you have about 40 years to participate and allow the compounding impact to work. A worker after 15 years with the equivalent of $31,000 after inflation amortized over the remainder of their life is about $150 dollars a month. A worker after 25 years with 70,442 could expect about $350 per month. A worker who participated 40 years with $176,649 could expect an annuity of $1,000 per month.

That means that the Bush plan mathematically only makes sense if you are between 20 and 30 years of age when you begin participating. It's important for every person to understand the results and the expected benefits. The Bush plan does not produce mathematically any significant contribution towards a workers retirement unless they can participate about 40 years in the plan.

All this still depends on finding the money, without borrowing which would add the interest costs, to replace the money diverted into the individual accounts and the money required to pay the benefits to all workers too old for the Bush plan.

Medicare and prescription drug coverage

Increase efforts to reduce medical costs waste and fraud without pushing the additional cost to either retirees or legitimate health providers.

Negotiate with drug companies to lower the cost of drugs by spreading the research and development cost to all purchasers not just American consumers.

Allow repurchase of American produced drugs from Canada.

Allow seniors to purchase insurance to cover gaps in their prescription drug coverage under Medicare.

Identify the funding source to pay for the prescription drug plan before taking effect in 2006.

Consider expanding the definition of Medicare income by including such things as interest income, dividends, stock options and tax exempt income to provide the added funding.

Trade deficit

We need to begin negotiating agreements that create a more level playing field. If we are to grant access to a foreign country's products into our markets, we must insist that our products have equal access to their markets. We need to confront China and any other country that manipulates their currency exchange rate in ways that impact the sale of our products in their country. At the present time, China sets its exchange rate at an artificially low level which makes their products cheaper and our products more expensive. This cannot be tolerated and only the market should be allowed to set exchange rates. We simply cannot ignore the ballooning trade deficit, which in calendar year 2004 is approaching $600 billion

Military

We need to evaluate our military force needs in light of our deployments and the potential risks that exist throughout the world

We need to evaluate our force structures to deal with the ever-changing threat to the United States.

We need to reconfigure the allocation of military units within the active forces, reserve forces and National Guard. The allocation of combat support and combat service support units has always been tilted toward the reserve and National Guard units. This has caused the requirement to activate guard and reserve units whenever active components are to be deployed for any extended period of time. The reason for this is that the combat support and combat service support units that the active component needs for extended deployments are located in the guard and reserve rather than in the active component itself. We need to make the active component, a reserve component, and the National Guard component more self-sustaining by distributing all types of units – combat, combat support and combat service support – to each of them. Utilizing National Guard and reserve forces should be to augment the overall force levels when a conflict demands manpower that goes beyond the available active component. They should not be activated to complete the necessary types of units needed for sustained combat operations of the active forces.

The policy of contracting combat support and combat service support functions to private contractors needs to be eliminated. This concept was intended to increase the level of combat forces available without increasing the overall end strength of the military.

Two problems have been documented from this policy. First, the salaries private contractors need to pay are substantially higher then we pay our military in order to attract the civilians to work in a combat zone. One example is that truck drivers in Iraq were receiving as much as $80,000 per year in salary which was far greater than the equivalent salary we were paying to military truck drivers. Add the overhead and profit for the private companies and the cost of providing combat support and combat service support functions via private contractors in a combat zone is actually greater than by just employing more military.

The second issue is that when the civilian contractors come under attack in a combat operation, they are unable to defend themselves and require the active military to divert resources in order to protect them. This is essential not only from a humanitarian standpoint but to also protect the services that they are providing such as logistics or food preparation.

Therefore the concept of contracting military support functions to private contractors has both increased our costs and created operational problems in the area of combat when these units come under attack by the enemy.

We need to discontinue development of the point-to-point anti-missile system. This system has an estimated cost of approximately $100 billion which does not count the large ongoing expense of maintaining and operating the system. The system has proven unreliable in almost half of the tests to date and provides very limited benefits in terms of a defensive system. First, the system can only be used against incoming missiles as a one time application. If the missile we launch does not disable or destroy the enemy incoming missile, there is no second chance option. In addition, the system cannot be used against other types of targets like water or ground targets.

The money from discontinuing this point to point missile defense system should be used to help develop the airborne laser system. This application utilizes a 747 as a generator and powerful laser weapon that can be used against incoming missiles on a repeated basis as well as on air, land or sea targets. It has far greater flexibility and application than the point-to-point Star Wars system and should be the primary anti missile weapons system.

We need to provide the necessary funding to bring our troops strength into alignment with our current and projected needs. At the present time the active component is insufficient to meet the missions it has been assigned and it needs to be brought to a level that enables it to meet its requirements with minimal or no use of reserve or guard forces. This needs to be done but not at the expense of new weapons development or in the replacement of equipment necessary for the active, reserve and guard components. It is clear we have not equipped our reserve and guard forces with the necessary equipment to enable them to meet their federal mission. This will require an overall increase in the defense expenditures to provide the manpower, equipment and training needed in the future.

Accelerate the repositioning of American forces from Germany, Japan and South Korea to the United States. Maintain pre-positioned stocks of heavy equipment and supplies to facilitate future deployments. This repositioning together with the increased troop levels of both the Army and Marine Corps will require revisiting the base closure planning to provide the needed facilities for the increased military stationed in the United States. Re-examine the airlift capability to enhance our ability to project ground forces into the areas of need in the future.

Illegal aliens

We should not allow legislation to pass that grants legal status to those who have broken our laws by illegally entering or remaining in the United States. We need a legal guest worker program that provides manpower needed to do jobs that cannot be done by Americans. The system should allow the needed manpower to enter the country, keep track of where they are and insure their return to their country of origin when the work is completed.

We need to staff our border patrol with both personnel and equipment to deal with the magnitude of the problem that faces us along our border with Mexico.

We need to control all those who visit the United States to ensure we know who they are prior to coming into the U.S. We need to make sure that they depart the United States when their authorized visit has ended.

Homeland Defense

We need to do more to close the loopholes that exist in our security system especially at our ports and small airports.

We need to fully fund the first responder elements with the equipment and training needed for them to do their job.

We need to fully fund all essential homeland defense requirements. It is not enough to tell the American public how much more we are spending but rather that we are fully meeting the needs to provide for homeland defense.

We need to enhance the cooperation with friendly countries to include intelligence, financial transactions, communications as well as police and law enforcement. The decentralized nature of terrorism in the world makes it impossible for any single country to effectively control the terrorist elements that would do them harm. It is in the best interest of every country that is threatened by terrorism to cooperate with each other in order to make sure that these elements are located and destroyed throughout the world. That does not mean we need to give up our sovereignty or our right to act but it does mean that we need an atmosphere of cooperation among countries to effectively control this growing threat.

The above are some of the specific actions needed to be taken to address the issues that face this country. There are certainly others that will need to be considered but these are the more essential issues that need to be addressed in the immediate future.

One final thought to consider. **The added interest you will pay because of the increased national debt under Mr. Bush will amount to over <u>$2 Trillion every 10 years.</u> That means every ten years you and your children <u>will pay increased taxes equal to the 2005 Federal Budget due to the fiscal policy of George W. Bush.</u>** Since 1980, the Americans have paid over $6.5 Trillion dollars in interest on the National Debt. That amount of money could have rebuilt all the infrastructure in the United States and made Social Security and Medicare financially secure. Per the Bush budget projections, by 2010, without the transition cost of Social Security, the gross national debt is estimated at $11.1 Trillion dollars! That will most likely require an annual interest payment of about $500 billion dollars or $1,500 per year for every man, women and child in America.

Section Three - Blogs from Bush Truth:

http://colgene.joeuser.com/

Background of Bush

Bush Trips Show His Stupidity and Arrogance

By COL Gene
Posted Monday, February 20, 2006 on *Bush Truth*
Discussion: Politics

Every week President Bush goes before pre screened audiences to pitch one of his policies. It could be his immigration policy or his tax policy or his energy policy or his solution to the lack of health care or his rational for wire taps or the Iraq war or how to fix Social Security. The results are the same-The vast majority does not want what Bush is selling. He believes by telling us again with different words that people will say, YES Mr. President. He does not seem to grasp it is the substance of what he is proposing not the SPIN or the audience he is addressing.

Some years ago I was a bank officer and learned that many bank vaults have "Time Locks" that prevent the vault from being opened during certain times. Bush is like a banker that goes to various banks at the times when the time locks will NOT allow anyone to open the vault door. He uses different combinations at each bank with the same result - The door does not open. WHEN WILL BUSH LEARN it is his MESSAGE that is the problem?

VERY BAD Day for the White House

By COL Gene
Posted Friday, February 10, 2006 on *Bush Truth*
Discussion: Politics

Today was a VERY bad day for Bush. Brown blasts the lack of response for help from Bush after Katrina. An Abramoff E-mail says he met with Bush a dozen times and that Bush even joked with him about his family. This was after Bush said "he did not know Abramoff". The VP told his former assistant to leak classified information to the press. Finally, the former CIA official Paul Pillar the 28 year veteran who coordinated ALL intelligence for Iraq said Bush Cherry-picked intelligence to justify the invasion of Iraq and that Bush had made the decision to invade Iraq aside from the intelligence. WHAT ELSE will become known about our president?

Bush Administration Tries to Silence TOP NASA Scientist

By COL Gene
Posted Sunday, January 29, 2006 on *Bush Truth*
Discussion: Politics

Dr. James Hansen, Director of the Goddard Institute for Space Studies said today that the Bush Administration attempted to stop him from talking about the need to reduce greenhouse gases linked to global warming. There are differences of opinion about this subject but the issue is the attempt of the Bush Administration to block this top climate scientist from providing his opinions on this subject. No matter what issue is at hand, this administration tries to stop any and all dissent from the position they take on a subject.

Dr. Hansen said he would ignore the restrictions that Bush is using to prevent him from speaking about this issue!

Tactics of President Bush

A Real Winner

By COL Gene
Posted Thursday, February 10, 2005 on *Bush Truth*
Discussion: Politics

In reviewing the strategy employed by President Bush it is clear that he has seized upon a tactic which has apparently worked well for him. That tactic is very simple, when the rationale you have used is shown to be untrue; you quickly shift to a new rationale.

Let's review a couple of Mr. Bush's decisions to enumerate this tactic. First was the Iraq war. The first reason was that Saddam Hussein and his weapons of mass destruction threatened the United States. We had things like a mushroom cloud, yellowcake, centrifuge tubes, mobile weapons labs and specific amounts of different types of biological and chemical weapons. When it became clear none of these were true, it was enforcing UN resolutions. Then it was Saddam was an evil dictator and we needed to free the Iraqi people. Today it is that we need to establish democracy in that part of the world so that it will spread throughout the region.

The next issue is the Bush tax cuts. The first rationale was that the American public was being overtaxed because Mr. Bush claimed we had a $5.7 trillion projected surplus. When it became clear there was no surplus, the rationale was to stimulate the economy. The problem with this rationale is that the majority of the deficit has been created by his tax cuts as documented by the Congressional Budget Office which last year estimated 270 billion of the $420 billion deficit was because of the Bush tax cuts. The new rationale being used to make the tax cuts permanent is that we need consistency so investors can plan properly. This is in spite of the fact that Brookings institute and others have estimated that making the tax cuts permanent will further drain the treasury and add another 2.4 trillion to the deficit by 2014.

The president and his political advisers have updated the quote from PT Barnum that "a sucker is born every minute" to a sucker is born every second. This can be the only explanation for the election results of 2004. I thought it was especially revealing that in this morning's business section the CEO of Hewlett-Packard was removed for failing to achieve the corporate objectives. The rationale used by many who voted for George W. Bush is that he screwed things up in his first term and needs to be reelected so that he can fix them.

And the Republicans called President Clinton, "slick Willy"!

Is George W. A strong leader?
Does he inspire unity and cooperation?

By COL Gene
Posted Tuesday, October 12, 2004 on *Bush Truth*
Discussion: Politics

When the voter during the second debate asked President Bush to name three mistakes he made as president, George W. displayed one of his greatest short comings - his inability to recognize flaws in himself, even when they are obvious.

In the 2000 presidential campaign, George W. pledged to restore more civility to American politics. Surely one of the mistakes that President Bush should have acknowledged to the voters question was that he had failed to achieve this pledge. In fact, he has made the rancor and political unrest much worse than at any time in modern times. Not since the American Civil War has there been more political unrest in America.

His failure to accomplish this is a clear indication of his inability to be an effective leader. His approach has done the very same thing with many people thought the world. Look at the reception he received when is addressed the U N last month - Dead Silence. The only applause came when he was about to leave the podium. It was as if their applause was to reflect his departure not at what he had to say.

The left in America hold George W. in distain. Most Democrats, if they are honest with themselves, will be voting against Bush more then for Senator Kerry. Their feelings are not because George W. is a Republican but because of his attitude and his total rejection of any positions that do not fit with the wishes of the conservatives. The right is just as bad or worse. People like Rush Limbaugh spew out their narrow minded positions at every opportunity. The conservatives can not complete a sentience without blasting the Liberals. They have only slightly less distain for the moderate Republicans, like me. If you do not support the conservative ideas you are stupid according to profit, Rush! He claims that he ties half his brain behind his back to make it fair to the Liberals. The truth is that if Rush had a brain twice its size, he could not complete a rational thought.

President Bush's answer to the question, name three mistakes you have made should surely have included his inability to bring cooperation and civility to American Politics. George Bush is strong but he is NOT a leader. A leader is one who has the ability to get people to go to a place they would not go by themselves. That is not George W. Bush. For that reason alone, America needs a change. We do not need another four years of divisiveness. We need a true leader that can unite America and enhance cooperation with the other nations of this world.

Branded by George W.

Pledges branded with hot coat hangers while George W. Bush was fraternity President

By COL Gene
Posted Thursday, September 30, 2004 on *Bush Truth*
Discussion: Politics
It keeps getting better and better. It turns out that Delta Kappa Epsilon applied hot branding irons made out of coat hangers to the backs of

pledges when George W. Bush was President of the Fraternity at Yale. The branding was done to 40 pledges and the hazing scandal was reported in the campus newspaper. The story was investigated and the fraternity was fined for the branding by the Yale Interfraternity Council. In a school newspaper interview with George W. Bush explained away the incident, saying "There's no scarring mark physically or mentally." Members of the fraternity that were branded when George W. was President still bear the mark today.

This story was investigated by the STAR newspaper when Bush was governor of Texas and he defended the illegal torture of the young fraternity pledges in the late 60's as a harmless prank. Looks as if George W. would be right at home in the prison system in Iraq!

More insight into George W.
Contact with the economics professor of George W. at Harvard

By COL Gene
Posted Thursday, September 30, 2004 on *Bush Truth*
Discussion: Politics

Yesterday I received a note and letters from Professor Yoshi Tsurumi, the economics professor of George W. at Harvard. Professor Tsurumi provided me two pieces of information that helped flush out the character of George W.

He provided copies of letters he wrote (published in The Scarsdale Inquirer) and one written by Nicholas D. Kristof of the New York Times. Mr. Kristof vetted the claims of Professor Tsurumi, who has been the victim of vicious attacks by the White House operatives.

The professor recalls a conversation with George W. one fall day in 1973. George was wearing a Guard jacket and the professor asked him how he got into the Guard. As we all know George W. answered with the "help of daddy and his good friends". The new information for me was a second statement by George W. when Professor Tsurumi asked George W. how he finished his National Guard commitment so quickly. The answer was "I got an early honorable discharge". The professor asked how he was able to do that and George W. answered," oh daddy had a good friend".

The second issue gets even more to what George W. is about. Professor Tsurumi vividly remembers George W. because of his outrageous statements such as,

"people were poor because they were lazy"

He opposed labor unions, Social Security, Environmental Protection, Medicare and Public Schools. To him the Federal Trade Commission and SEC were unnecessary hindrances to "free market completion".

The policies of FDR were socialism.

He showed his lack of compassion for the ordinary working Americans.

Does this sound like a "Compassionate Conservative" to ANYONE? Does this sound like the teachings of the Christian faith George W. professes?

The professor does provide some very interesting insight into the man who would be reelected President.

The real issue about the Bush National Guard Service
What does it mean today?

By COL Gene
Posted Sunday, September 26, 2004 on *Bush Truth*
Discussion: Politics
As usual, the political drones, as well as the president avoid the real issue about the National Guard service of George W. Bush. The focus is on the CBS documents not the truth of the president's service and his truthfulness about that service today.

First is how Bush got into the Guard. He contends he got in through his own merits. That has been shown to be untrue. The former Speaker of the Texas House, Ben Barns has admitted a friend of the senior Bush asked him to get George W. into the guard. The president's former professor at Harvard, Yoshi Tsurumi, has come forward and told CNN that George W. admitted his father had a family friend get him into the Guard to avoid service in Vietnam. In addition, his flight aptitude test scores have been found and George W. scored in the bottom 25% and would never have been sent to flight school and given a direct commission without the help of Ben Barns. George W. was also placed ahead of 100 other young men that did not have the pull George W. had. In spite of all this, President Bush does not come clean as to how he got into the Guard and that is the real significance in 2004.

The same problem exists with the President's fulfillment of his responsibilities to the Guard. Although CBS used documents that were not authentic, the facts were TRUE. Lt. Bush failed to take a required physical and was grounded. The tax payers spent lot of money to train George W. to be a pilot and when he did not obey regulations and lost his ability to fly, he DID NOT MEET HIS RESPONSIBILITY. He did not obey Air Force Regulations and it does not matter where he was attending drills. In addition, his commander's secretary stated that George W. Bush was ordered to take the required physical by LTC Killian. The pay records of Lt. Bush show for five months he did not attend the required monthly drills at ANY LOCATION. His Officer Efficiency Report confirms Lt. Bush did not attend drills. The policy at that time for members of the Guard and Reserve that did not attend drills was for the member to be put on active duty. George W. was allowed to miss drills with no penalty. Today George W. says he met his responsibilities and he received an Honorable Discharge. It is true he some how received an Honorable Discharge but he did not meet his obligations or obey the regulations when he did not get a physical and attend required drill.

If the members of the military today did the same things as Lt Bush, we would not have an effective military. There is nothing more important to a military organization than for the members to obey their orders. In 2004, our Commander -in-Chief is not telling the truth about how he got into the Guard or the fact he did not fulfill his obligations or obey the oath he took when he was commissioned!

TIME Outed Rove and Libby

By COL Gene
Posted Thursday, July 21, 2005 on *Bush Truth*
Discussion: Politics

The articles in Time this week have clarified a number of issues that have been bouncing around Joe User. The first issue is the status of Valerie Plame in the CIA. Many bloggers on Joe User have claimed she was not a covert CIA Agent. The CIA, in a very unusual action, confirmed that Valerie Plame was in fact an NOC covert agent. This is agents who works undercover without the protection of any diplomatic immunity and are the agents in the most danger for themselves and the contacts that they develop in living their double life for the CIA. These agents are difficult to establish and are the type of agent that was intended to be protected under 1982 Intelligence Identities Protection Act. Unfortunately, this law was designed to be very difficult to violate and the one thing that the Time articles did not address is whether Rove or Libby met all the technical requirements that violated this particular statute.

The second issue that was clearly documented in the Time articles was the fact that it was Karl Rove that first identified Wilson's wife as a CIA operative to Matt Cooper of Time magazine. It was not another reporter, it was Rove. In addition, Rove told Cooper Valerie was involved in the WMD which has also been confirmed by the CIA. In addition, Matt Cooper testified before the grand jury that Scooter Libby, the vice president's chief of staff, confirmed the fact that Wilson's wife was a CIA operative working on WMD. It is now clear that the two White House staff members mentioned in the Bob

Novak article which identified Valerie Plame as a CIA Agent were Rove and Libby.

These two individuals consistently lied saying that they were not involved with identifying Wilson's wife as a CIA agent. It is likely that President Bush was unaware at the outset that Rove and Libby were the White House staffers that outed Plame given the fact that Bush said he would fire the persons responsible for identifying Plame as a CIA agent. No one knows exactly when Bush and Cheney learned it was their principal assistants that had loose lips but Bush has now changed the criteria to being convicted of a crime not merely violating the spirit of law which was to protect agents such as Valerie Plame.

Time magazine has done us a great service in identifying Rove and Libby as liars who endangered one of our CIA Agents. In addition to the potential harm to Plame, there is the danger to people Valerie Plame worked with while she lived her secret life as a covert agent. That is why the CIA went to the Justice Department and a Special Prosecutor was appointed. It is also the reason that the FBI is conducting a major investigation of this matter. Only Patrick Fitzgerald, the Special Prosecutor will be able to determine whether Rove or Lobby actually violated the complex law intended to protect the identity of clandestine operatives in the CIA. There is no question that Rove and Libby are the people that violated at least the spirit of law and lied to the American people. It is time for President Bush to follow his original commitment to terminate Rove and Libby for their actions in identifying one of our covert CIA Agents.

Budget/Economic Policies

Bush 2007 Budget is Unbelievable
Our President has lost his mind!

By COL Gene
Posted Sunday, February 05, 2006 on *Bush Truth*
Discussion: Politics

Bush is getting ready to send his 2007 budget proposal to Congress. While Bush is pushing to make his tax cuts for his wealthy supporter's permanent, look at some of the proposed CUTS he has included in his 2007 Budget:

Cuts from Education
Cuts from the Dept of Energy
Cuts from the National Institute of Health
Cuts from Centers for Disease Control
Cuts for Medicare Reimbursement
Cuts for food aid to CHILDREN under 6 and the ELDERLY
Cuts for the NATIONAL GUARD and ARMY RESERVE

Given his statements about the need for education, the potential problems with health and a possible pandemic, the plight of the poor he identified in his New Orleans Speech and the situation with our military being under sized, these budget cuts are as wrong as they could be. Rather then increase the Federal revenues to help balance the budget Bush is proposing cuts in ESSENTIAL elements of the government. The cuts in the National Guard and Reserve have raised a firestorm with the nations Governors as well as the Congress. 75 Senators sent a letter to Bush Thursday saying HELL NO. I doubt that most of these ridicules cuts will be approved, especially in an election year. The real question is HOW COULD WE HAVE ELECTED A PRESIDENT THAT IS SO OUT OF TOUCH WITH WHAT IS NEEDED IN AMERICA?

Gene P. Abel, Colonel, USAR Ret.

U S Economy NOT Improving for the American Family

By COL Gene
Posted Thursday, January 19, 2006 on *Bush Truth*
Discussion: Politics

Yesterday the Dept of Labor reported that after inflation, the Average Hourly Earnings DROPPED .5% in 2005. That followed a .7% drop in 2004. Thus, during the past two years the Average Hourly Wage has DROPPED 1.2%. That means that for the average family the economy is WORSE not BETTER as Bush and company claim. The report said, "People see energy prices going up and they get a little worried about what they can afford to spend". Analysts said the wage weakness was having an impact on consumer confidence. This coupled with record high credit card balances being carried by the average American family show the Economic Boom that Bush claims is taking place is an illusion for the average American! The only place where a Boom is taking place is on the income statements of SOME companies such as Big Oil and in the net worth of the wealthy!

What is the 800 Pound Gorilla in the Federal Budget?
And it's not Social Security, Defense or Medicare

By COL Gene
Posted Monday, February 14, 2005 on *Bush Truth*
Discussion: Politics

President Bush ignores the real problem and potential solution to this country's fiscal morass which is the interest on the national debt. The rationale used to mitigate the increasing debt is that it is the same % of GDP. The real issue is not the percent of GDP the national debt represents but how much interest does that debt require us to pay.

Since 1980, American taxpayers have paid $6.5 trillion in interest on our national debt. That amount of money would have solved both Social Security and Medicare funding problems as far as the eye could see. The ongoing interest comes off the top of our tax dollars

82

and is in the $330 billion range in the 2004-05 budget. That money would pay for prescription drugs, increased national and homeland defense expenditures, education, and still leave room for another tax cut.

The real issue is that the worst is yet to come. Interest rates are at a 45 year low and when they return to their historic norms, the interest payments will skyrocket to as much as $500 billion per year. The interest payments never end until we repay the debt. If you look at the Bush Budget on the OMB web site, you will see he is telling the American taxpayers that by the time he leaves office we will have a national debt of $10 trillion. When he took office that number was $5.7 trillion. When Ronald Reagan took office that number was $909 billion or an increase of 11 times from 1980 to 2008.

The issue with the federal budget is not cutting social programs, increased defense expenditures or the impact of the baby boomers (Social Security and Medicare). It is the growing interest on the national debt. The policy we are following does not stop adding to the national debt and will not reduce the interest we will be required to pay year after year. Until we face up to the fact that we must pay for what we are spending there is no solution and in time the debt and the interest obligation it carries with it is going to swamp the American economy.

Bush Budget Shows Where His Heart IS
St. Luke, Ch 12:34

By COL Gene
Posted Monday, February 07, 2005 on *Bush Truth*
Discussion: Politics

The unveiling of the Bush budget is the clearest indication of where Bush and his compassionate conservatives place their values. The budget shows either reduced funding or cuts in numerous areas which will have a negative impact on America. A sample of his cuts or reduced funding include:

Cuts in home heating assistance for the poor – Let them freeze to death

Medicaid - Healthcare for the poor – Let them die in agony

Subsidies for growing cotton, rice, corn, soybeans and wheat – No help for the Blue States

Money to help repair our dams - Let them flood us out

Elimination or reduced funding for programs to help educate our children to include: Vocational Education, drug-free schools and literacy programs – From the Education President

Lack of funding to pay for the new border guards Bush proposed - The hell with homeland defense.

These are just a sample of the150 areas Mr. Bush has chosen to reduce the budget deficit. At the same time, his budget fails to include the $80 billion that he is asking for the Iraq War or any money for his Social Security private accounts. Next year comes the $50 billion for the Bush unfunded prescription drug benefit!

At the same time Mr. Bush is proposing to cut things that will have a negative impact on millions in our country, he wants to make his tax cuts permanent, especially those that benefit his wealthy supporters. Think of it, Bush wants to make permanent tax cuts for people making six and seven figure incomes while he cuts assistance to heat the poor people's homes, help the poor pay their medical bills, educate our children, repair our dams, help our farmers, protect our boarders, etc. Mr. Bush has clearly documented what is said in St. Luke chapter 12 verse 34, "For where your treasure is, there will your heart be also".

For a president who wears his religion on his sleeve, I suggest Mr. Bush pick up his Bible and read what his Lord Jesus Christ had to say about helping the poor and how difficult it is for a rich person to enter Heaven. St. Luke, Chapter 16 versus 20 through 31 is a good passage. That is the story of the servant Lazarus, who received almost nothing from the rich man and when they died, the rich man looked up from hell seeking help from Lazarus who was in heaven.

I for one do not use biblical citations very often but given the fact that George W. Bush continually references his Christian faith, I think he should reexamine his priorities in light of the teachings of the Savior he professes belief in! Those teachings would rescind the tax cuts for the wealthy to help the poor and eliminate the deficit.

God save the United States of America!

Bush plan to cut deficit in half is bankrupt

By COL Gene
Posted Wednesday, January 05, 2005 on *Bush Truth*
Discussion: Politics

One of the Bush objectives for the second term is to reduce the annual deficit by 50%. That would mean by 2008, the United States would still be running an annual budget deficit of over $200 billion every year. There are many who believe other objectives set out by President Bush such as making the tax cuts permanent, changing Social Security with even more debt and paying for his prescription drug plan will make even cutting the deficit in half impossible.

Even if he somehow can manage to cut the annual deficit in half the country has lost. When George W. Bush took office the total federal deficit stood at $5.7 trillion. By the time he leaves office it will be at least $10 trillion. His objective of cutting future annual increases in half does not deal with the issue that he and his predecessors since 1980 have created the $ 10 Trillion debt. Many people believe that this is just a BIG number. When interest rates returned to their historic norms and the treasury is forced to pay these rates on the huge debt that has been created, the impact of what Mr. Bush and Mr. Reagan have done will be clear.

In 1980 we embrace this idiocy whereby we cut taxes and increase spending thus creating a structural deficit. George W. would have us believe the deficit is because of 9/11 and the recession. The truth is we have run a deficit in 21 of the last 24 years because we refused to bring our tax revenue equal to our spending. In 1980 the national debt stood at less than $1 trillion. Reagan added three trillion, George H. W. and Clinton added another 1.7 trillion and George W is well on his way to add another 3.3 trillion for a total of $10 Trillion by 2008 if Bush keeps his promise.

Our objective should be to create a $ 200 Billion annual surplus to be applied to the total debt. To repay the roughly $10 trillion in debt that will most likely be on the books when George W. Bush retires to Texas, it will take the United States 30 years at $200 billion a year to repay the deficit created by our irresponsible fiscal policy. Even the Bush supporters will be dismayed when they see how much annual interest has increased and what it will due to their taxes in the future! That increased interest will come off the top and will take the money we need for Medicare, Social Security, education, national defense and the rebuilding of our infrastructure which is falling apart as we speak. The objective of George W. Bush, even if he cuts the annual deficit to $200 billion annually is a bankrupt tax and fiscal policy for the US. The interest could reach $500 Billion per year which is more than we spend on National defense. That interest will never end until we repay the debt which can not even begin under the Bush policy!!!!! The Bush objective of a $200 Billion dollar deficit needs to be changed into a $200 Billion surplus. That makes Bush about $400 Billion off the mark EVERY YEAR. Not bad for a Harvard MBA!

Is Bush trying to "Starve the Beast"
If so, it may backfire!

By COL Gene
Posted Saturday, October 02, 2004 on *Bush Truth*
Discussion: Politics

"Starving the Beast" is a theory that says, the conservatives are creating a financial crisis by drastic cuts in taxes with sizeable increases in spending. Professor Paul Krugman of Princeton is one who talks about this idea. This theory says the purpose of creating this fiscal crisis is to attack Social Security and Medicare which many conservatives hate. It is doubtful President Bush is the author of this idea but may be the means for conservatives to make it happen.

Whether the fiscal crisis we are creating is due to "Starving the Beast" or some other reason like GREED, it will be of little consequence. The harm it will cause will be the same!

I believe the reaction to our impending fiscal crisis will not be to make significant cuts or eliminate either Social Security or Medicare. These two social programs are by far the most popular programs ever created by congress. In addition, only the wealthy could live out their retirement years without these programs paying the expected benefits. Any real change to either program would have to be very far out so as to not impact the current voting population.

If the conservatives, as a reaction to a future fiscal crisis, were to attempt to be actually cut or eliminate either of these programs, they will be swept from power. Then the moderate and liberal majority will impose their solution to the crisis and keep Social Security and Medicare in place. Some possible solutions they may employ come to mind:

End the cap on Social Security Wages ($87,700 this year) and tax all earned income the same as Medicare. This would only impact the wealthiest 10 % of Americans.

Include all earned, tax exempt, dividend and capital gain income to the tax base for Medicare. This would only impact the wealthy.

Increase the tax rates for the top two income brackets and use the added revenue to solve the fiscal crisis.

These are but a few ways to solve the problem and make sure the wealthy pay the bill.

I guess it would be good for the conservatives, regardless of the motivation for the current fiscal and tax policies to remember this saying: BE CAREFUL WHAT YOU ASK FOR!

Charge and Spend policy of the conservatives

By COL Gene
Posted Wednesday, September 29, 2004 on *Bush Truth*
Discussion: Politics

One of the most destructive policies of President Bush and his conservatives in Congress is the fiscal policy we are following. This policy is to drastically cut tax revenue while increasing spending. The result is a structural deficit. This began for real in 1980 with the Reagan tax cuts and spending increases. It is true, tax rates prior to 1980 were too high and some reduction was needed to stimulate the economy. However, the extent of the cuts and the size of the spending increases started the United States on a path that will produce catastrophic financial problems. George W. has reinstated these same policies.

Let's review some facts. To save a question as to the data I will use, I will provide the source as I go.

Source: Dept of the US Treasury, bureau of public debt via the Web:

Debt at 1980 was $909 Billion and the interest in the Federal Budget was $90 Billion in FY 1980.

By the end of the Reagan term the debt was $4 Trillion

By the time George W. took office the debt was $5.7Trillion

Today the debt is $7.5 Trillion. The interest on that debt is about $340 Billion.

Since 1980 the Federal Government ran a sizeable deficit in 21 of the past 24 years since we began the Supply side Economics of Reagan - Voodoo Economics

During the past 24 years the American taxpayer has paid $6.5 Trillion in interest and over 40% is paid to foreign individuals or corporations.

Per the budget projection of George W. Bush which is found at the OMB website, by 2008, if President Bush is reelected in November and continues his fiscal policy, he predicts the national debt will stand at just under $10 Trillion in FY 2008 and we will be running an annual deficit in 2008 of $250 Billion.

Now the Bush supporters say this is all manageable. They also blame the deficit on 9/11, the Iraq war and corporate misconduct. The truth is that the deficit began for real in 1980, a few years before 9/11/2001 and the largest contributor this year, about $270 Billion of the $450 billion, is from his tax cuts per the Congressional Budget Office. Now George W. wants to make all his tax cuts permanent which per a study by the Brookings Institute will add yet another $2.4 Trillion to the deficit by 2014. Why should Americans care about the size of our Debt?

The debt creates a mandated expenditure in the federal budget. The reason why Bush and his conservatives have been able to get away with taking the national debt from, less than a trillion to 7.5 Trillion is because the interest rates have been at a 45 year low. That enabled the treasury to finance the growing national debt without a large increase in the annual interest. That is about to come to an end. As interest rates return to historic norms, the ability to pay the interest each year will become impossible. If interest rates return to their historic norms by 2008 when Bush predicts the National Debt will be about $10 Trillion, we could have an annual interest obligation of $500 Billion each and every year. That is more than George W. projects we will be spending on national Defense or on all other non military discretionary expenditures. Every cent of that 1/2 Trillion in interest buys us NOTHING! It does not pay for our defense, education, health care, transportation - NOTHING. What that interest pays for is the past when we spent more then we taxed.

If that is not bad enough, at no time does the Bush fiscal policy ever create a balanced budget. If he is successful in making the tax cuts permanent, the situation gets even worse and by 2014 the Brookings Institute study shows we could have a National debt in excess on $13 Trillion. Even if we come to our senses today, it will take a Herculean effort to balance the budget and generate the Trillions in surplus to repay the national debt to significantly lower the annual interest required!

I have been a moderate Republican for over 40 years, I believe we must be willing to pay for what we want or want less. That is not what George W. and his conservatives are about. That is why I will vote for Senator Kerry to break the hold the conservatives have on the purse strings. Bush tells us that will bring just more spending than - Not so as long as the Republicans hold control of either house of Congress. We need a moderate policy. One that does not create more spending but does not make the current tax cuts permanent. By 2011, the tax rates will return to the levels they were in the 1990's. That was the period of the greatest sustained growth in our history and when the wealthiest Americans did better than any other economic group! When I hear the conservatives say that the tax rates in the 1990's were oppressive, I ask how then did the wealthy and the middle income Americans do so well under those tax rates?

The Fiscal policy we are following is passing a debt to our children and grandchildren. That debt and the interest it will require, added to the financial burdens of the Baby Boomer generation retirement is a disaster in the making. As large as our economy is, it can only handle so many multi-Trillion dollar problems. We need to restore the fiscal sanity of the old GOP, the one that wanted a balanced budget amendment. We can not survive much more of the so called Republican conservatives if we are to remain strong and FREE!

Bush understates budget deficit

By COL Gene

Posted Wednesday, February 23, 2005 on *Bush Truth*
Discussion: Politics

The final budget deception is that even the President's projected deficit of $10 Trillion by 2008 is understated by trillions of dollars. The reason the actual deficit is understated is because the budget deficit is calculated using an accounting trick called the "Unified Budget".

The unified budget combines the Federal Budget with Social Security and Medicare. At the present time, both Social Security and Medicare show an annual surplus. They both collect more in taxes then they pay out in benefits. This will come to an end as the baby boomer retirements increase.

In 2003, a comparison of the deficit using the Unified Budget calculation with the Federal Budget, without Social Security and Medicare, was completed using data from the Congressional Budget Office by the Center for Economic and Policy Research. It clearly showed the impact of combining Social Security and Medicare with the Federal Budget. In 2003, the deficit reported by the Bush administration, using the Unified Budget method, showed a deficit of $400 Billion. Looking only at the Federal Budget, the 2003 deficit was $600 billion.

The study concluded that the tax cuts left the budget seriously out of balance and calculated what it would require in spending cuts or tax increases to bring the 2003 budget into balance without Social Security and Medicare. To balance the 2003 Federal Budget alone would require spending cuts of 36.1% or tax increases of 56.6%.

The only reason to distort the true federal deficit by adding the surpluses from Social Security and Medicare is to make the deficit appear smaller. When Social Security and Medicare no longer are generating an annual surplus, the true size of the Federal Budget Deficit will become clear. This process is like taking the income and expenses of two brothers and combining them. One brother spends far more then he earns while the other earns more then he spends. Together they may look fine but the true financial condition of each brother is distorted.

$675 Billion Deficit if FY 2005
The Bush Lie

By COL Gene
Posted Thursday, February 24, 2005 on *Bush Truth*
Discussion: Politics

President Bush has been understating the size of the Federal defect. He has been using two main distortions to accomplish this lie. First, he understates the cost of the War. Bush included 35 Billion on a line called "Proposed Supplemental" when he knows the costs per year are more then $80 Billion. That is a $50 Billion dollar understatement.

The second method of understating the federal budget deficit is by adding the annual surplus in Social Security and Medicare to the Federal Budget which lowers the deficit. That distortion is about $200 billion per year. Thus the REAL 2005 deficit is closer to:

As stated by President Bush $427 Billion
Understatement of war 47 Billion
Social security/Medicare Surplus 200 Billion

_____

ACTUAL 2005 Budget deficit $ 674 Billion

If the President was required to certify the Federal Budget statements, like corporate executives under the new law he asked Congress to pass, he would be in violation of that law! However, that law does not apply to the President of the United States.

FISCAL CONSERVATIVES ABANDONING BUSH

By COL Gene
Posted Friday, June 10, 2005 on *Bush Truth*
Discussion: Politics

More and more fiscal conservatives are coming to realize the fiscal policies of George W. Bush are anything but conservative. A search of Google will provide many articles about the problems fiscal conservatives are having with President Bush. Some fiscal conservatives like the Federal Reserve Chairman, Alan Greenspan and former Secretary of the Treasury, Paul O'Neill have always counseled fiscal conservatism and a balanced budget even if it meant ending tax cuts. Other more dogmatic Republicans have tried to find excuses for the enormous deficit by blaming it on the war in Iraq, the war on terrorism and economic slowdown at the end of the Clinton administration. The truth is none defense spending has increased by about 6% per year during the Bush administration and so we have the worst of both worlds - a huge increase in military and defense expenditures coupled with a large increases in other spending.

For the true fiscal conservative the current situation brings the realization that deficit is so large that it cannot be solved without major increases in federal revenue. Thus, for the fiscal conservatives to achieve a balance between expenditures and revenues they will

93

be forced to accept tax increases no matter how many cuts are made to deal with the huge deficit. If you exclude the Social Security and Medicare surpluses and look simply at the federal expenditures compared with the federal revenue, the imbalance is $675 billion in FY 2005. Even when the Iraq war has come to an end, we are looking at as much as $600 billion imbalance between the federal expenditures and the federal revenues. Solving the fiscal morass that has been created over the last five years is going to be painful and especially for those who believe in fiscal conservatism.

WHY THE GROWING ECONOMY ISN'T HELPING THE AVERAGE AMERICAN!

By COL Gene
Posted Tuesday, August 09, 2005 on *Bush Truth*
Discussion: Politics

The Bush administration claims the economy is growing. It is true statistics show that corporate profits are increasing and there has been some job and GDP growth. The fact remains that the areas in which the economy is growing are not affecting the average person.

Recent studies have shown during the past year, the average price of homes has increased 20% while wages for middle income workers have increased only a few percent. The result is middle income Americans are worse off today in terms of being able to purchase a house. The same thing is true for health care and the increase in energy prices. The impact on the majority of Americans from this so-called growing economy is that they are worse off even with the economic growth. The middle income workers are worse off because their wage growth has not kept pace with the increased cost of healthcare, housing and energy. The poor have had NO wage growth. The group of Americans that are better off are those that receive a great deal of their income from dividends. Corporations have increased their profit margins and are paying larger dividends. The problem is that has not helped the middle income or poor Americans meet their day-to-day living expenses.

Especially problematic are the increased energy costs. They are MUCH worse then taxes increase because they impact the poor, the middle income and the wealthy alike. Tax increases generally do not impact the poor. It is no wonder why the polls show that most Americans do not approve of the way Bush is running the economy. The reality of the economic growth is it is NOT helping the poor and middle income Americans who are worse off today than they were in January 2001.

Energy Policy

Bush Defense of Exxon Profits DEAD WRONG

By COL Gene
Posted Thursday, February 02, 2006 on *Bush Truth*
Discussion: Politics

Yesterday George W. Bush defended the huge profits of Exxon in his speech in Nashville. He said they were justified because they were the result of the market. The AP article went on to mention that after all Bush was a former oil man from Texas. What the AP did not mention is that the two oil companies Bush ran went bankrupt while he was in charge. Only a fool would rely of the statements of someone with the track record of Bush about running oil companies.

The truth is that BIG OIL does not respond to the market they manipulate the market. They do not need to increase their market share to increase profits or have big productivity increases. The oil companies have every right to increase the price of their end product because of price increases they incur. What the oil companies are doing is using the unstable crude oil prices to not only recover there added cost but add to their profit. If crude oil prices increase and that would add $.20 per gallon, the oil companies jack up the prices by $.50 per gallon. That negatively impacts EVERY COMPANY and EVERY PERSON in this country and our President tell us that is fine!

If I were the President of Harvard University and knew some where in the White House there is a diploma saying Harvard granted George W. Bush an MBA, I would be ashamed! Every American that is being priced gouged by the oil companies should write Bush and tell him how wrong it is for him to defend such actions. Congress needs to tax away that added profit and invest it in research and production of ways to make America less dependent on oil!

Solve the Energy crises

By <u>COL Gene</u>
Posted Saturday, February 05, 2005 on <u>Bush Truth</u>
Discussion: Politics

Restore the Café standards and make them apply to all cars, trucks and SUVs.

Establish new targets for increased miles per gallon for each type of vehicle over the next 10 years.

Establish tax credits for car manufacturers who achieve the established standards.

Establish tax surcharges to car manufacturers who fail to meet the new mileage standards.

Utilize the additional tax revenue from surcharges to help fund the tax credits to corporations who achieve the new Café standards.

Provide federal subsidies to more fully utilize available coal supplies to create the energy needed wherever possible. Subsidies should be used to help provide for clean air equipment and to research new methods of utilizing coal in a non polluting way. Tax credits should also be used to convert existing oil and gas fired generators to coal and with the cost of transporting coal from the source to the user.

Provide subsidies to help car manufacturers develop cars and trucks using alternate propulsion systems such as fuel cells and hybrid/electric vehicles.

Provide subsidies to develop long-term renewable energy supplies including geothermal, wind, direct solar conversion, cold fusion, fuel cells etc. The objective would be to reduce our dependence on foreign oil as well as provide for the sale of the new technology and equipment to other countries. This would have the obvious advantage of not only solving our energy problem but eliminating many of the political entanglements that our dependence on Middle East oil creates. In addition, a reduction in the purchase of foreign oil would help our balance of trade as we sell the new technology and equipment to other countries. Thus this strategy would be a win-win-win-win situation for our country by enhancing employment, corporate profits, reduce our trade deficit as well as simplifying some of our political entanglements.

Encourage the development of natural gas in areas controlled by the United States

Encourage the development of additional oil supplies that are under the control of the United States and do not endanger the environment.

Carefully evaluate any new or renewed agreements to provide United States produced energy to other nations. Our objective should be to first provide for energy independence before pledging our assets, especially oil and gas, to other countries

Gene P. Abel, Colonel, USAR Ret.

Iraq War

Bush Plan to Rebuild Iraq Riddled with Waste and Fraud
Bush former campaign workers at fault

By COL Gene
Posted Monday, January 30, 2006 on *Bush Truth*
Discussion: Politics

The results of the first Audit of our Iraq rebuilding program were released by the U S Inspector General for Iraq. The deficiencies are astounding. Tens of Millions of our tax dollars were totally wasted. The issues include both incompetence and fraud. The auditors found the inexperienced American Officials including workers from the Bush election campaign are responsible. In one program dealing with rebuilding oil revenue auditors were unable to account for $97 Million of the $120 million dollar project. The auditors concluded, those deficiencies were so significant that we were precluded from accomplishing our stated objectives.

Another example of how George W. Bush abused his power to appoint political cronies that were incapable of meeting the responsibilities of the offices to which they were appointed by Bush! Another FEMA!

Bremer told Bush more troops needed for Iraq
Bush to Bremer - Don't worry about it

By COL Gene
Posted Tuesday, October 05, 2004 on *Bush Truth*
Discussion: Politics

Everyday more and more becomes public knowledge about Iraq. The CIA, in response to a request from VP Dick Cheney, undercuts the rational of Bush and Cheney that there was a connection between Saddam Hussein and al-Qaeda. This is a separate conclusion from the 9/11 Commission. Today reports were released that Former Ambassador L. Paul Bremer acknowledged that we did not have enough troops in Iraq and that he told President Bush we needed more troops. On Monday night Ambassador Bremer addressing a group in Sulfur Springs, W. VA said, when he arrived in Iraq May 6, 2003 he found "horrid" looting and a very unstable situation. "We paid a big price for not stopping it because it establishes an atmosphere of lawlessness" "We never had enough troops on the ground" Bremer said. He also said that he pleaded for more troops with President Bush. When the White House was asked about this, Scott McClellan would not confirm that Ambassador Bremer had asked Bush for more troops.

President Bush has told Congress and the American People that if he had been asked for more troops they would have been provided. We now have the chief US Administrator in Iraq telling us that was a lie. We now have President Bush failing to take the advice in the planning stage as to the troops required when the Army Chief of Staff told Bush it would take several hundred thousand, "boots on the ground". Now we have information that shows the President failed to provide the forces required when the War was underway and lied to us when he said if more troops were required they would have been provided. This is the "strong Leadership" we are asked to return to the White House as the Commander-in-Chief for another four years.

It will be interesting to see how President Bush and his "SPIN DOCTORS" try and discredit, Ambassador Bremer, the man in charge during the Iraq War!

Iraq becomes terrorism training ground
Per the Sec. of Defense and CIA Director

By COL Gene
Posted Thursday, February 17, 2005 on *Bush Truth*
Discussion: Politics

Yesterday the new CIA director, Porter Goss told a select Senate committee on intelligence that Iraq has become a terrorist training ground. He further admitted that he could not guarantee that the Iraqi insurgents have not have stolen enough nuclear material from Russia to create a weapon. Today Secretary of Defense Rumsfeld noted it is likely the United States would again be attacked by the Islamic extremists. In addition, we now have a partnership between Syria and Iran which is the result of what they perceive as a threat to them from the United States.

I would like to understand how 1,450 lives lost in Iraq, 25,000 injured in the $300 billion dollars we have committed has made us safer given the comments of the CIA Director and the Secretary of Defense? For those who continue to argue the Bush decision to attack Iraq was a wise decision, please explain the assessments from Rumsfeld and Goss. It is a shame the president cannot admit when he has made a mistake. I think the clearest indication of this weakness is that even today with the knowledge that there was no WMD or connection to 9/ 11 Bush still contends he would've done the very same thing. I can not understand how the American people can accept such a position that the Iraq War has made us safer given the reality on the ground and the assessments of Secretary Rumsfeld and CIA Director Goss.

BUSH HAS ABANDONED MILITARY VICTORY IN IRAQ

By COL Gene
Posted Friday, August 12, 2005 on *Bush Truth*
Discussion: Politics

The strategy at the White House has changed with respect to the Iraq War. We are now attempting to withdrawal just as soon as we have trained enough Iraq security and military forces. Bush wants to make the withdrawal appear legitimate and when that magic number has been achieved, you will see the troops begin to come home. The truth is we are not winning the military battle against the insurgents. Our military fight and die to secure an area and a few months later the very same elements are operating in that area. We then repeat the action and loose more of our troops. We do not have the manpower to control the entire country and prevent the reintroduction of the insurgent forces in the areas that we cleared with our precious military lives.

When the history books are written about this conflict, it will not be a positive oration. First, the rationale for the war was untrue. Bush supporters will say everyone thought there was WMD and therefore he did not lie as to his reason for attacking Iraq. The problem with that rationale is that the reason given today is to provide the Iraqi people the right to choose their own government. If that were the reason we chose to depose Saddam Hussein, that is the reason that Bush should have provided the Congress of the United States before asking for approval of the war resolution. Bush did not give that reason and this whole process was justified by the imminent danger to the United States. Then Bush said it was to enforce the UN Resolutions however the UN NEVER made the United States or England the enforcement agent for UN resolutions. Another rational Bush gave to remove Saddam was to rid the world of an evil dictator. There are many more evil dictators that exist in this world and Saddam Hussein was not the worst of the lot. If you have any doubt about that, look at what is happening to millions of people in Africa. If we were to provide this choice of the type of government that Bush NOW claims is the reason for the war, why not Cuba 90 miles from Florida? Why not Syria, North Korea, Iran, China or a host of other countries where the people do not have a choice. Why not our so-called ally, Saudi Arabia.

The real reason Bush wanted to invade Iraq may never be known. It was clear that this was in Bush's mind when he first took office. The removal of Saddam Hussein was a discussion item at the VERY FIRST Cabinet meeting. This has been clearly stated by the former Treasury Secretary Paul O' Neal. This was before 9/11, before we were attacked or heard about the War on Terrorism in America. The lesson we must learn is that in the future if a president asks Congress to go war with reasons that are not as stated, that president needs to be impeached and removed from office. If George W. Bush had asked Congress for authorization to attack Iraq so that Iraq people could select their own form of government, the resolution would NEVER have been approved. It is a sad day for this country that our president did not give the actual reason for America to go to war. The Bush LIE has cost America over 1,800 lives, more then 25,000 injured and over $300 billion dollars! It has created thousands if not millions of NEW enemies all over the world!

THE UGLY TRUTH ABOUT THE IRAQ WAR

By COL Gene
Posted Sunday, October 02, 2005 on *Bush Truth*
Discussion: Politics

Today the Philadelphia Inquirer has a story by Tom Lasseter about the situation in Iraq which is more accurate and anything we are hearing from the Bush administration. The interview is with two 3rd infantry division snipers serving in Iraq. They described their day-to-day life in this struggle and have come to some very disturbing conclusions.

The bottom line for these two sergeants who have served over 7 years each in the Army including multiple tours in Iraq are as follows: Quote the reason why they are fighting us is not Osama bin Laden. They are fighting us because we are here. They just want us to leave. I guess that would be a victory for them. In past situations you had a good guy and a bad guy and the troops were impassioned, but now troops just want TO GO HOME.

How different is THIS ACCOUNT of the Iraq War from what we are being told by Bush and his minions. The truth, I fear, is MUCH closer to what these two battle hardened soldiers are saying then what President Bush is telling the American people.

Bush is a Buffoon

By <u>COL Gene</u>
Posted Thursday, December 15, 2005 on *Bush Truth*
Discussion: Politics

Yesterday George W. Bush, out of his own mouth, documented that he is a Buffoon!

For the very first time he admitted he took this country to war, the most important decision any president can make, based on faulty information. These are the Presidents own words, "It is true that much of the intelligence turned out to be wrong. As President I'm responsible for the decision to go into Iraq."

That would have been an important admission had Bush stopped there. However what followed is hard to believe. His next statement was, "Saddam was a threat and the American people and the world is better off because he is no longer in power."

If the information that said he was a danger was incorrect as the President admitted, how was Saddam a threat? What possible justification for going to war existed with a country that did not have the means to be a threat? There are many tyrants in this world that wish others harm. They are NOT a threat if they do not have the means of being a danger.

Even when Bush admits he was wrong, according to him he was right. How foolish Bush make himself look. This great country deserves a leader that can take responsibility for their mistakes not one that acts like GWB.

JOBS

Bush Policy on Education is a TOTAL Inconsistency

By COL Gene
Posted Friday, February 03, 2006 on *Bush Truth*
Discussion: Politics

Yesterday Bush told us that Americans must become more competitive. He went onto say the way to achieve that was through education. At the VERY SAME TIME, Bush and the conservatives passed the budget cuts which reduced the money for student loans and increased the interest rates on these loans making it HARDER for students to get the additional education Bush claims is the KEY to be competitive! In addition, since the passage of his signature policy called, No Child Left Behind, his budgets have UNDER FUNDED his OWN requirements for this program by over $20 Billion Dollars.

WHY does Bush not see how stupid he looks by undercutting the very solution he claims is necessary to solve the problem of American competitiveness?

Job Creation

By COL Gene
Posted Saturday, February 05, 2005 on *Bush Truth*
Discussion: Politics

This week the Bureau of Labor Statistics has released the net bottom line on job creation during the first Bush term in office. According to the Bureau, 119,000 net new jobs were created during the four years of the Bush first term. During that same four year period, over 5 million Americans entered the work force seeking jobs.

The retort is that the president doesn't create jobs. The truth is the economic policy of the federal government has a great deal to do with economic growth and in fact job creation. President Bush is constantly telling us we need to judge by results. I fully agree with the president on this point and so for his first four years, President Bush deserves an F in job creation.

For the economy of our country to make up for the last four years plus create the jobs the growing population will need during the next four years, we will need to produce 250,000 jobs each and every month between now and January 2009 to be at the very same place we were when George W. Bush took office. Let's compare the actual job creation each month with our need to create these 250,000 jobs per month to see whether or not the economic policies being followed by this administration are meeting the needs of our citizens.

Medical

Bush Health Savings Accounts NO ANSWER

By COL Gene
Posted Wednesday, February 01, 2006 on *Bush Truth*
Discussion: Politics

The State of the Union Speech did demonstrate that George W. Bush has a basic understanding of some of the major issues facing America. The biggest domestic issue however, the growing Federal Deficit was not addressed.

One major issue Bush offered a solution for was healthcare. He acknowledged the problem of escalating costs and the fact that 46 million people HAVE NO COVERAGE. His solution is to shift health coverage to be paid for by the individual with before- tax earnings. This plan will encourage even more employers to drop company paid health coverage and shift the cost to the working family. This is where President Bush is simply out of touch with the reality. The Median family income in 2005 was $44,000 per year, which means many families live on far less to arrive at that Median amount. The average working family lives from pay check to pay check and is NOT saving anything. The savings rate in America is the lowest since 1933 and in December 2005 was negative which means people went into their past savings to pay for their current expenditures. The bottom line is that tens of millions of families DO NOT HAVE the money to place into the proposed medical savings accounts. The Bush suggestion is NOT AN ANSWER for the middle or low income families.

We need to make Bush look at workable solutions to the problems he seems to recognize and to recognize issues like the deficit that he has yet to acknowledge.

Lets cut Medicaid

By COL Gene
Posted Sunday, February 20, 2005 on *Bush Truth*
Discussion: Politics

This week the governors came out against the proposal by President Bush to cut $40 billion from the budget for Medicaid. That program pays for health care for the poor and disabled and is funded jointly by the Federal and state governments. Therefore, when the Federal Government cuts funding to the states those cuts must be made up by the states.

If President Bush is successful in cutting the funding to states for Medicaid, the states will then begin looking within their budgets to see what monies can be rearranged to pay for the reduced funding. One tactic which states have used is to shift monies from public education which is one of the largest state expenditures. If the states choose to make up the federal funding loss in Medicaid by shifting expenditures, the problem rolls one further step down hill to local school districts. At this point the funding problem has no where else to go and local taxes go up.

The bottom line is taxes, whether they are federal state or local can only come from the taxpayers. Shifting the problem is not solving the problem. We need to take an honest look at our social and non-social needs and then come up with the funding necessary to pay the bill.

The way we have been acting, is similar to a person who needs to buy a gallon of milk for their family. They shop around and find the best price is $3.00 and they go to purchase the milk. Our hypothetical person has only $2.50 and the store manager explains the milk is $3.00. The person pays $2.50 in cash and charges the other $.50 to their credit card. This goes on day after day, week after week, year after year until the day when the hypothetical taxpayer discovers he can't pay his credit card bill. At this point they throw up their hands and declare bankruptcy.

Improve efficiency to save money

By COL Gene
Posted Wednesday, March 02, 2005 on *Bush Truth*
Discussion: Politics

The Bush proposal to cut $40 billion from Medicaid before savings are realized would jeopardize the health care for the poorest Americans was the message that came out of the Governor's conference this week. President Bush made the case that the growing Medicaid expenditures must be reduced. There was agreement to look for ways to streamline Medicaid, reduced fraud and lower the cost of prescription drugs. One example is that some elderly Americans are transferring assets to their family to qualify for Medicaid. This practice must be dealt with to help stem the rising costs. Medicaid will pay for 53 million of the poor and disabled for an estimated cost of $329 billion.

The governors were clear; to make the proposed cuts in the Federal Budget before savings are realized can not be absorbed by the state budgets. Therefore rather than simply cutting the appropriation as Mr. Bush has suggested, it will be necessary streamlining Medicaid first and producing the savings before cutting the Federal contribution. There were signs that the governors understood the impact of this growing expenditure and the need to addresses the problem but made Mr. Bush understand simply cutting the Medicaid appropriation as he is proposing simply transfers the problem from the federal to the state budgets. One factor which is increasing Medicaid costs is the loss of health care by lower paying jobs. It is doubtful, given the catastrophic impact on every state budget, that the cuts proposed by Bush will make it through Congress until savings have been realized.

Military

Pentagon Study Shows Bush is Destroying the Army

By COL Gene
Posted Wednesday, January 25, 2006 on *Bush Truth*
Discussion: Politics

Yet another study that documents the American military is being over utilized and that the strength of the Active Army is too small for the current deployments. In the 2000 Campaign Bush acknowledged the Military was too small and that was BEFOR the Iraq war. After becoming Commander-in-Chief he ignored the needs of our military and made the problems even greater.

The study concludes the Army is a thin green line that could snap. There are still some that are actually looking at yet another flash point in Iran.

http://www.cnn.com/2006/US/01/25/army.study.ap/index.html
WASHINGTON (AP) — Stretched by frequent troop rotations to Iraq and Afghanistan, the Army has become a "thin green line" that could snap unless relief comes soon, according to a study for the Pentagon. Andrew Krepinevich, a retired Army officer who wrote the report under a Pentagon contract, concluded that the Army cannot sustain the pace of troop deployments to Iraq long enough to break the back of the insurgency. He also suggested that the Pentagon's decision, announced in December, to begin reducing the force in Iraq this year was driven in part by a realization that the Army was overextended.

A Disgruntled Military

By COL Gene
Posted Wednesday, December 08, 2004 on *Bush Truth*
Discussion: Politics

The complaints from our military to the Defense Secretary today are the latest in an unhealthy trend with our military force. Secretary Rumsfeld listened to the complaints from our soldiers in what appeared to be a big surprise for him today. This follows the refusal of a reserve unit to obey orders because they lacked the proper equipment. If also follows the statement of a National Guard General that his troops did not have the proper equipment.

Complaints about inadequate equipment, the stop loss policy that is disrupting the lives of both are active military and reserve forces as well of the extensive use of National Guard and reserves clearly document that both Bush and Rumsfeld failed to plan for the Iraq war. The secretary told the troops "you go to war with the army you have". The problem with that statement is that the United States chose when we went to this war. Why did we go to war without the necessary equipment and the manpower we need?

It the 2000 election, George W. Bush indicated that the army was too small and needed to the increased. He spent the last four years doing nothing to correct the problem that he himself identified. The Iraq war is not like World War II or Korea when the timing was forced upon us but rather we went to war against a country that was not threatening us in a preemptive fashion. It is time that the President of the United States and the Secretary of Defense is made to explain why they chose to go to war without the necessary equipment and manpower. The lack of both has added to American casualties. We are approaching 1,300 dead; about 9,000 combat injuries and almost 15,000 non-combat related injuries. This war has killed or injured 25,000 young Americans. How many of these are because our Commander-in-Chief took our military to war improperly prepared?

Army and Marine Corps do not meet Recruiting Goals!

By COL Gene
Posted Thursday, March 03, 2005 on *Bush Truth*
Discussion: Politics

Today the Department of Defense reported that first-time in a decade United States Marine Corps failed to meet its recruiting goals in both January and February by a total of 275 recruits. In addition, The United States Army fell short of its recruiting goals by almost 2000 recruits in February

There was concerned expressed by the results in recruiting both active, reserve and National Guard soldiers given the increased demand for military recruits. Although some of the shortfall is because of the improving economy, other factors such as the Iraq war, parents who are discouraging their 18 year olds from enlisting are substantial reasons why the recruiting goals are not being met.

The Bush policies of extending the tours of active and reserve personnel, reported shortages of equipment for both the active and reserve components and the mounting casualties and injuries in Iraq are beginning to show in the recruiting effort.

Policies of Bush

Our President is OUT of Touch
He is not Tone deaf he is Stone deaf.

President Bush has said he will veto any attempt by Congress to stop the proposed sale of six American Ports to Dubai Ports. Mr. Bush has asked what is the difference between a British company who currently owns and operates the ports and a company from the United Arab Emirates? Let's take a look Mr. Bush:

The current operator is NOT owned and operated by the British Government.

Dubai Ports is OWNED and OPERATED by the UAE.

None of the 9/11 terrorists were English citizens.

Two of the 9/11 terrorists were from UAE.

England recognizes Israel.

UAE does NOT recognize Israel.

Funding for 9/11 did not go through British Banks.

Funding for 9/11 did go through UAE Banks.

England did not warn Osama bin Laden in 1999 of our intent to capture him which enabled his escape but UAE DID WARN HIM and that prevented his capture by the United States.

England does not support Islamic Terrorist organizations.

Several Islamic organizations have been supported by elements in the UAE. The UAE was only one of three countries in the world that recognized the Taliban as the ruler of Afghanistan.

President Bush tells us that the security at our ports will remain unchanged under this new contract. That means we will continue to inspect about 5% of the containers that come into the United States. **That also means Dubai Ports will be responsible to supervise loading ALL these containers and prepare the documentation showing what is in all these containers.** This is what Mr. Bush is willing to turn over to the UAE.

Mr. Bush – Congress and the American people DO NOT WHANT THIS CONTRACT APPROVED! Just like Rep. Myrick ® from NC said when she wrote you about allowing this contract to be approved

– Not only NO but HELL NO! Mr. Bush - bring on your Veto.
Congress - override his veto.

It is time for Congress to insist that George W. Bush begin to meet
his responsibilities to FULLY protect our ports and borders. He
must request to fully fund the Coast Guard and our military. It is
DISGARCEFUL how Mr. Bush has FAILED to fully protect our
country. **It is time for an American company to own and operate
our ports.**

Out of Touch with America

By COL Gene
Posted Monday, March 07, 2005 on *Bush Truth*
Discussion: Current Events

I watch the Lou Dobbs show and each night he has a question that
listeners respond to via the Internet. I know these polls are not
scientifically constructed however the topics that are being covered
are in the forefront of the issues that are important to our nation.

It's remarkable to me night after night those who choose to vote on
these polls show the overwhelming disapproval of the policies our
government is following. What is most astounding is that the results
are not even close - 80, 90 & 95% oppose the policies being followed
by Washington.

It doesn't matter if the question is on foreign policy, the economy,
homeland defense, Social Security, the results are the same, and the
overwhelming majority is against the policies that we're following in
this country. I wonder if the leaders of Congress and President Bush
take note of these opinions that are aired night after night

KATRINA SHOWS THE BUSH PRIORITIES ARE ALL WRONG!
America needs a change

By COL Gene
Posted Monday, September 05, 2005 on *Bush Truth*
Discussion: Politics

This disaster and its impact on New Orleans and the Gulf coast was not only predicted but there were detailed plans prepared showing what needed to be done to strengthen the levees around New Orleans and the coastline along the Mississippi river. These studies and simulations were prepared in 2001 and 2002 for the Bush administration. They were almost 100% accurate as to the consequences of failing to rebuild this infrastructure in the largest port in the United States. George W. Bush ignored these studies and the warning contained in them.

The studies clearly indicated what it will take in terms of rebuilding the levees to withstand category four and five hurricanes as well as repairing the coast line along the Mississippi. The cost to rebuild the region would have been in the $20-$30 Billion range according to the studies. Bush, rather than starting to implement this essential rebuilding, actually cut the funding for the Corps of Engineers to that region beginning in late 2001. He diverted the money to the war in Iraq. The truth is that our priorities are DEAD WRONG! With 10% of what George W. Bush has spent in Iraq, we could have completely rebuilt the levees in New Orleans and the Mississippi coastline and prevented this disaster from occurring. Now we need to rebuild an area as large as Great Britain and still need to repair the levees and the Mississippi coastline. The cost in human lives and dollars are many times what it would have been if Bush had his priorities in line with the NEEDS of this country!

In addition, water levels are rising because of the global warming and here again the Bush administration has done nothing to protect our environment and ignores a growing problem that the use of fossil fuel is helping to create. Rather than seek alternate energy sources with the hundreds of billions of dollars that we are dumping in the Iraq War, we ignore our energy needs. There are studies that show the infrastructure of the United States is aging and that it will take more than $1 trillion dollars to repair all the levees, bridges, roads, electrical grids, dams, schools, and water and sewer systems throughout this great nation. There is NO money for these needs but we have SPENT 1/3 of what it would cost to rebuild the infrastructure across the entire United States with what we have spent in Iraq. The time has come to redirect the priorities in America to meet the long term needs of our people and not the political ideology of the conservatives in this country! Bush cuts the federal revenue with tax cuts and ignores essential repairs. He starts a war that did not make us more secure and spends the money needed to help rebuild America on that war. WAKE UP AMERICA!

IF THERE IS ONE USEFUL THING KATRINA HAS DONE, IT IS TO SHOW HOW WRONG THE BUSH AGENDA IS FOR AMERICA!

Why are there so many poor?

By COL Gene
Posted Saturday, September 24, 2005 on *Bush Truth*
Discussion: Politics

Reading many of the JoeUser posts one would think that ALL the poor are by CHOICE. It would be useful to look at the poor and determine the real reasons they are poor not just- it is their choice or fault.

The reasons would include:

Lack of will
Age
mental or physical capacity
Available jobs

non-living wage jobs
Natural disaster i.e. Katrina

Looking at the reasons WHY would not produce the simple answer - It is the fault of the poor that they are poor. These storms have shown just how many poor there are in this country and how little these people have to meet the BASIC needs of life. We should help all the poor except for the LACK OF WILL group. Even the people in the LACK OF WILL group need to be encouraged to change their outlook

Bush Policy of Spreading Democracy

By COL Gene
Posted Sunday, September 18, 2005 on *Bush Truth*
Discussion: Politics

The highly publicized election in Afghanistan yesterday has documented the fatal flaw in the foreign policy George W. Bush is pursuing which is, the Spreading Democracy Theory. This is the Holy Grail of foreign-policy which is supposed to make America safer and for which we are willing to sacrifice our young men and women.

The problem with this idea is that in many areas of Afghanistan, the voters DID NOT KNOW any of the candidates running for office. At the polling places, voters talked among themselves as to who each was going to vote for since no one knew any of the candidates. They did not know what they stood for and might as well have closed their eyes and voted. The reason for this is the candidates were afraid to campaign or make themselves known for fear of assassination. This is the very same thing that has taken place in many locations in Iraq. Many candidates in the highly touted Iraqi election were not known until the voters saw their names on the ballot FOR THE FIRST TIME when they voted! George Bush does not realize that the Muslim populations in these countries are simply not ready for democracy. Until there is security, that will allow candidates to make themselves and what they stand for known to the voters, there can be NO REAL DEMOCRACY! We are not even close to that in either Iraq or Afghanistan!

1984 arrived 17 years late in 2001
Bush is "BIG BROTHER" according to the New York Times

By COL Gene
Posted Saturday, December 24, 2005 on *Bush Truth*
Discussion: Politics

Today the New York Times answered the question of WHY BUSH IGNORED THE 1978 F.I.S.A. law. What is taking place at NSA is eavesdropping on millions of calls and E-mails with sophisticated computers that harvest those calls and E-mails that meet the patterns that the NSA has established. The messages that are selected by the computer systems are then monitored by analysts to determine if they are harmless or contain information relating to our security.

Thus, the statements by Bush and his senior aids that stressed the executive order allowing warrant less surveillance was limited was untrue. The NSA, under the President's secret order, has become Big Brother. The number of total calls and E-mails monitored by the computers at the NSA most likely number in the millions each day. Calls analysts review which the computers identify of potential interest could be in the thousands each day and the limited number acknowledged by Bush are those analysts actually listen to in detail.

Now we know WHY Bush was so unhappy when the New York Times first ran this story. WE also know WHY Bush is not obtaining warrants under the 1978 law. The volume is so great, warrants either before or within 72 hours is impossible. The only practical way they could in part comply with the law is to seek warrants for those messages the analysts believe have security implications AFTER THE FACT.

Power, Arrogance and Money

By COL Gene
Posted Wednesday, December 21, 2005 on *Bush Truth*
Discussion: Politics

Today the news documents what may be signs that America is in trouble. Cheney tells us that we need to expand Executive Power and defends the Bush actions of failing to obtain court orders to spy on Americans. Bush claims that his authority as Commander in Chief of our military gives him the power to ignore the law. The AP learned that Tom DeLay received 48 visits to Golf Clubs, 100 flights in corporate jets, 200 stays in world-class hotels and 500 meals at restaurants where dinner for two is about $200 - ALL this paid by corporations that want access and special treatment from our government.

Defenders of the system will claim that has been part of politics in the past which is true. However, the level of the corruption and arrogance of power has NEVER been as great as it appears today. When one group has control with almost absolute power, that power corrupts absolutely.

GOP with the Help of Cheney are the Grinch for the Poor

By COL Gene
Posted Thursday, December 22, 2005 on *Bush Truth*
Discussion: Politics

The Christian conservatives did it again with the passage of the 2006 budget:

Cut 255,000 low income families from food stamps.

Cut basic aid for food to the poor by $700 million

Made changes in Medicaid that will allow states to impose substantial co-pays and fees on the poorest people for their health care.

Cut Billions from child support.

Two weeks earlier this same group cut taxes $90 Billion for the wealthiest Americans.

Merry Christmas to all and to all a good night!

Social Security

Bush doesn't get it on Social Security

By: COL Gene
Posted: Monday, March 21, 2005
Discussion: Politics

President Bush continues his romp across the country telling seniors not to worry about their benefits under Social Security. What he doesn't understand is that seniors are concerned not simply for their own benefits but for the benefits of their children and grandchildren. They do not want the uncertainty of the stock market for Social Security. Poll after poll shows that the vast majority of Americans do not support private accounts.

It is not necessary to establish private accounts to ensure the solvency of Social Security. Even some Republicans have admitted that President Bush made a drastic error when he placed the private accounts as the principal issue before the American public. The principal issue is not private accounts it is the solvency of Social Security. The truth is that carving out trillions of dollars from the Social Security trust fund by establishing individual accounts actually makes the financial situation worse not better for Social Security.

As one of those seniors, I am not concerned about my benefits. I am concerned about the benefits for my children and grandchildren. I believe the place for private accounts invested in equities is over and above Social Security. We need to fund the existing Social Security plan so that the money will be there for my retirement and the retirement of my children and grandchildren. We also need to make sure working Americans understand they need something more than Social Security for retirement. Individual Equity Accounts should be in addition to Social Security and NOT part of Social Security.

Let's Fix Social Security

By COL Gene
Posted Wednesday, February 16, 2005 on *Bush Truth*
Discussion: Politics

President Bush continues his discussions across the country about his change to Social Security. The Social Security question has two basic components. First, is the philosophy of what Social Security is and what it should be for workers in America? Second, is the mechanics of how to maintain the solvency of Social Security?

Social Security has always been a guaranteed minimum retirement benefit for the American worker. Something that was predictable and guaranteed. The problem with the Bush solution is that it alters the basic philosophy of Social Security. What George W. Bush is proposing is to convert the floor into an elevator. There is no question that individual equity accounts hold the potential of increasing a worker's retirement but it also holds the possibility of having less should the market be down at the time of a worker's retirement. There is a place for individual equity accounts and that place is over and above the minimum guaranteed floor of Social Security. Therefore, we should maintain the philosophy of Social Security as a guaranteed minimum and encourage workers to create individual equity accounts during their working life IN ADDITION to Social Security.

If we are to maintain a guaranteed minimum for Social Security, we need to fund the system through the bubble of the baby boomers. At the present time, 3 1/2 people are working for every one receiving benefits. At the present time, the taxes being collected are more than the benefits being paid out. Because of the baby boomers that will change starting in about 2018 and there will be only two people working for each person receiving benefits. When the baby boomer bubble has passed (in about 70 years), the system will right itself and return to a relationship similar to what exists today. Therefore, the issue is to finance retirement benefits under Social Security for the huge increase in population that occurred after World War II. That should be done by increasing the Social Security Trust Fund so it can bridge the funding deficit created by that bubble.

There are two suggestions that have been made to help fund the Social Security deficit. One is to augment the trust fund by General fund revenues which will require us to first balance the budget. The second idea is to extend the income limit on Social Security wages (currently the first $90,000 of earned income) the same as the Medicare tax. That would cause many billions of additional tax dollars to flow into the Social Security Trust Fund. That additional money could then be invested in equities to augment the yield to the trust fund over and above the 3% that the treasury bonds are currently paying on bonds held by the trust fund. This concept has been successfully used in EVERY state pension plan in the United States. Why would we not duplicate a successful strategy that is keeping our state pension plans solvent for Social Security?

The American people need to contact their Senators and Congressman to tell them that they want to maintain the minimum guaranteed Social Security system and have it funded by increasing the Social Security tax limit and investing that additional money in a sound mix of equity investments. Although some might benefit from the equity accounts proposed by President Bush, I believe the guaranteed Social Security income is far more important to the vast majority of Americans! Every American worker should let Congress know how they feel. This is not a decision that should be made by the president or congress without knowing what the America people want.

SNOW JOB ON SOCIAL SECURITY
And MEDICARE

By COL Gene
Posted Thursday, March 24, 2005 on *Bush Truth*
Discussion: Politics

Yesterday the trustees for Social Security and Medicare issued an update as to the health of these two programs. The report clearly shows that the American public has been given a "snow job" by John Snow, Secretary of Treasury and George W. Bush.

The report shows that the real crisis is not Social Security but Medicare. According to the report, by 2020 the Medicare Trust Fund will be depleted and Medicare will be able to pay only 79% of claims. The Social Security Trust Fund will be depleted in 2041 and Social Security will be able to pay only 73% of Social Security benefits starting in 2041.

Therefore, what we are seeing is that the crisis President Bush and Secretary Snow are telling us about is in the wrong program. It is true that both Medicare and Social Security need long-term funding changes but the real crisis is Medicare. To compound this SNOW JOB take a look at Medicaid which is in crisis NOW? Funding for Medicaid is a joint venture between the Federal and state governments. President Bush and Congress have proposed cutting $40 billion out of the Medicaid appropriations next year and dumping it in the laps of the state governors who told President Bush they are unable to replace this cut in funding from state budgets.

We need a Secretary of the Treasury like Paul O'Neil who advised the President of the facts, not helped the President distort the facts.

Save Social Security from George W. Bush!
Let's consider some added ways to fund the system!

By <u>COL Gene</u>
Posted Thursday, January 06, 2005 on *Bush Truth*
Discussion: Politics

Another major priority of the Bush administration appears to be Social Security. President Bush and his staff have been closed mouth as to the exact proposals they plan to recommend. Now the camel's nose is beginning to appear under the tent.

First we heard that the 2% diversion of worker Social Security taxes to private accounts might be recommended. That was immediately followed by where is the money to come from to allow Social Security taxes to be diverted into private accounts? Again the answer begins to appear by Mr. Bush saying no tax increases to pay for the transition cost to partially privatize the system. Now we are hearing a 4% option which would double the amount of the transition funds required and again no real explanation as to where these monies would come from.

Within the last several days we have heard about increasing the retirement age and cutting back benefits more significantly in the out years to pay for the transition costs. That also seems to imply that Bush intends to borrow the transition costs and repay them at some future time by reduced payouts and increased retirement age. Who will pay the interest on any borrow transition funding? In other words it looks as if he is proposing the very same solution he has for everything else and that is borrow and pay some time in the future.

Many people believe that the federal government misspent some of their Social Security taxes and that is the reason why the trust fund is not large enough to cover the baby boomer retirement. Some years ago, I obtained my parents Social Security lifetime statements and compared the amount of tax they and their employers paid over the years with the money they received from Social Security. This analysis made it crystal clear why the Social Security trust fund is not large enough to deal with the baby boomers. Although my parents were covered by Social Security from its inception my mother in the 18 years that she drew Social Security received 20 times more in benefits than both she and her employers paid into the system. My father, who received Social Security for 26 years, got about 27 times more money than he and his employers paid into the system.

So before we become too critical of how our Social Security taxes have been used lets take a look at who has received them. No investment, including the Bush equity plan for Social Security, would have generated the income necessary to pay 20 to 30 times the amount contributed to the system. In fact when I looked at my parents Social Security statements I found that during the 30s 40s 50s and 60s the amount paid into the system was very small. Thus, even if it had been invested in equities the way George W. Bush is suggesting, they still would not have had nearly enough money to receive what they got from the Social Security System. In addition, where would the account maintenance fees come from? That is certainly a question that needs to be asked of President Bush. For the small taxpayer even today, an investment of five or six hundred dollars per year will see a great deal of the added income that Bush is touting as a solution paid to investment bankers. How will that help the workers making an average income? Today the White House admitted that the creation of the individual accounts Bush wants will not solve the funding needs of Social Security.

We should be looking at other ways to resolve the funding issue with Social Security. All we're looking at is what Bush proposed. When the President selected the members of the Social Security Commission he made sure all the members shared his notion of the individual accounts and other possible suggestions were not considered. Below are specific alternative suggestions to provide the funding necessary for Social Security without borrowing more money:

Stop any attempt to extend Social Security benefits to illegal aliens.

Continue the gradual increase of full retirement to age 70.

Consider limiting the payout to retirees with non-Social Security income above $150,000 per year. When a retired couple has non-Social Security income above $150,000 per year (index this amount each year by cost of living), the benefits under Social Security would end at the point when the individual's contribution had been completely returned to the taxpayer. For example, if an individual during their lifetime paid $70,000 in Social Security taxes, excluding their employer contribution, their Social Security payments would terminate if their non-Social Security income exceeded the maximum amount when they reach a total payout of $70,000 in this example.

Should a retiree's non-Social Security income fall below the maximum amount, the Social Security payments would resume based on their original entitlement so long as their non-Social Security income remained below the maximum amount.

Re-examine the option to set aside 2% or 4% of their Social Security tax to individual accounts. Issues to be evaluated should include:

Evaluate whether or not the creation of these individual accounts will make Social Security solvent. If the creation of these individual accounts does not solve the funding issues of Social Security, then why create massive change to the existing system? Look at the Transition costs to supplant the removal of the younger workers 2 % or 4% of their taxes into individual accounts. Develop realistic estimates as to the transition costs. Identify the source needed to fund this transition amount before deciding to implement this change without borrowing more money.

Consider the impact on a worker who selects the private account option wherein the value of their account at the time of retirement was less than the total benefits that would be paid under the traditional Social Security amount. Would there be a provision to subsidize the payment of the amount received under the individual retirement option to bring it equal to the traditional Social Security benefit?

Evaluate an alternative to the individual equity account that would allow portions of the Social Security Trust Fund to be invested in stock market index funds. This would provide the advantage of increased earnings equity investments produce without the high cost to maintain millions of small accounts that would be required under the individual account concept. This idea has been successfully used by every state pension fund of the United States as well as many large corporate pension plans. Lift the income limit upon which Social Security taxes are paid to include all earned income similar to the current Medicare tax. This additional revenue would increase the Trust Fund and with the higher earnings from investing in equities should fund the system without borrowing more money.

Taxes

Bush/Cheney 1040's prove Rich NOT overtaxed
The boys did good for themselves with the tax cuts

By COL Gene
Posted Saturday, April 16, 2005 on *Bush Truth*
Discussion: Politics

The 1040's for Bush and Cheney are on the web. Here are the results from their tax returns:

In 2004 Bush had taxable income Line 35 of $784, 219 and paid 26.4% in Federal Income tax. In 2001 Bush before his tax cuts he had taxable income of $811,100 and paid 30.8 % in Federal Income taxes.

The Big winner is Cheney. In 2004, he had taxable income of $1,734,373 and paid 21.3% in Federal Income taxes. In 2001 Cheney had taxable income of $4,356,635 and paid 38% in Federal Income Taxes.

The more you make the less you pay after the Bush tax cuts. The President is in the top 3% and Cheney the top 1% of wage earners. ANYONE THAT BELIEVES THAT PAYING 21% OR 26 % IS TOO HIGH FOR PEOPLE MAKING THIS AMOUNT OF INCOME, HAS LOST THEIR MIND! SO MUCH FOR THE CLAIM THE RICH ARE OVERTXED!

BUSH NEEDS TO INCREASE TAXES

By COL Gene
Posted Saturday, September 03, 2005 on *Bush Truth*
Discussion: Politics

The disaster created by Katrina should be the focal point for President Bush to acknowledge the federal tax revenue is insufficient to meet the overwhelming needs in the United States. The devastation created by this storm will surpass any natural disaster in our history. It has destroyed over 90,000 square miles and displaced more than 1.5 million Americans.

The resources that will be necessary to rebuild this region as well as the ongoing needs of the 1.5 million people who have no jobs, no homes or anything else, will require a major commitment of resources that do not exist within the Federal Budget. We can not just hand out money that does not exist!

Prior to this disaster, the United States was running an unacceptable deficit and the aftermath of Katrina should make it clear that now is the time to change they way we are managing the financial affairs of the United States. The magnitude of this disaster together with the existing deficit mandate that the federal government increase the revenue to meet those needs. George W. Bush needs to take a lesson from his father who raised taxes and from Ronald Reagan who raised taxes when the need was clear. There are NO cuts that can pay for this huge undertaking.

In the past, when we have had major disasters and wars, the country increased taxes to pay for those needs. We must restore this region and the port facilities which will require not only rebuilding homes but the entire infrastructure in this area of the United States. If George W. Bush will not admit his fiscal plan for this country is not working, it is time for the Congress of the United States to act. They need to make it clear to Bush that if he will not be part of the solution Congress will pass the needed legislation over his objection. NO MORE EXCUSES- We MUST provide the needed funding to pay for the restoration of this region and pay for our other needs without borrowing any more money!

A 15 % FLAT TAX
Who gets What?

By COL Gene
Posted Monday, September 26, 2005 on *Bush Truth*
Discussion: Politics

Some Joe Users believe a 15% flat tax is the way to go. I still do not know how much such a tax would produce in Total Federal Revenue to see if that would balance the budget. However, this is what it would do to couples filing jointly and claiming the standard deduction in 2004 if they made $20,000 and $35,000 compared with the Bush/ Cheney taxes:

Income of $20,000 would pay **$500 more**

Income of $35,000 would pay **$700 more** .

Bush would pay **$86,000 less.**

Cheney would pay **$ 109,000 less.**

NOW WE KNOW WHY THE WEALTHY WANT A FLAT TAX

Unemployment

Unemployment Rate does not give a clear job picture!
Added 262,000 jobs and the unemployment rate goes UP

By COL Gene
Posted Friday, March 04, 2005 on *Bush Truth*
Discussion: Politics

The employment numbers today were a step forward by producing 262,000 new jobs. Not only is that more than were expected, but it is more than economists claim are necessary to keep pace with population growth. To keep pace with our growing work force, our economy needs to produce about 125,000 new jobs each month. Thus, last month we produced more than double that amount. Most would believe that would result in a reduction of the nation's unemployment rate when in fact the unemployment rate increased from 5.2 to 5.4%.

We have seen months in the past when almost no jobs were created and the unemployment rate went down. Thus it is clear; the unemployment rate statistic is not giving us a clear picture of job condition in our country. What we should be doing is producing monthly, the number of Americans who do not have jobs that pay a living wage. It should include all people who need a living wage job that do not have such a job and compare that statistic month-to-month see how well we are doing in creating meaningful jobs for our growing population.

Sources:

Against All Enemies by Richard A. Clarke

Alan Greenspan, Chairmen Federal Reserve

Bill Gates

Boston Globe-Bush National Guard Service

Brookings Institute

Center For Economic And Policy Research

Charles Lewis

Congressional Budget Office - CBO

Dan Rather

David M. Walker Comptroller General of the United States

Dept. of Labor, Division of Labor Force Statistics

Department of the Treasury, Bureau of Public Debt

Face The Nation Interview with VP Cheney 2001

Federal Reserve

General Accounting Office –GAO

General Barry McCaffrey

General Eric Shinseki, Former Army CoS

Gene P. Abel, Colonel, USAR Ret.

General Wesley Clark

Hoover Institute

Imperial Hubris by Anonymous (Michael Scheuer)

Journal of Foreign Affairs

Lt. General John Riggs

Lt. George W. Bush's National Guard records

Office of Management and Budget – OMB

Paul Craig Roberts

Paul O'Neil, Former Secretary of the Treasury 2001-2003

Paul R. Pillar retired CIA Top Counterterrorism Coordinator

Plan of Attack by Bob Woodward

Popular Science — Airborne Laser

Presidential Commission on Social Security

Professor Jeffrey Record — United States Army War College visiting professor

Professor Paul Krugman, Princeton University

Professor Rogan Kersh

Senator Ted Kennedy comments on Medicare January 2005

Sierra Club

Social Security and Medicare Trustees

The Price of Loyalty by Ron Suskind

Toshi Tsurumi, Harvard Professor of GWB

United States Army War College

U S Conference of Mayors

Warren Buffet

Washington Post

60 minutes

60 Minutes II

About the Author

Gene P. Abel is a person that is not satisfied with the status quo and has always been in the forefront of change. He was born in Allentown, Pennsylvania in 1941. Mr. Abel is from a German and Scottish heritage and was educated in the public school system. He earned a B.S. from Penn State in finance/economics and an MBA from Lehigh University. He was a distinguished military graduate and received a regular army commission as a second lieutenant in the field artillery branch of the Army in 1963. Abel served as a nuclear weapons officer in Germany and a member of the nuclear release authority that begins with the President and ended with Lt Abel. Upon the completion of his tour in Germany, he spent two years as a finance officer at Ft Lewis, Washington. After four years of active duty he accepted a reserve commission as a Captain in the Army Reserve and left active duty in 1968.

He remained in the Army Reserve until 1993 and retired at the rank of Colonel. He is a graduate of the Army War College and was awarded numerous medals including a Meritorious Service Medal on two occasions. He was promoted to Colonel after only 19 years of service and was nominated for promotion to general officer soon after completing the Army War College. However, his lack of combat service, which is most likely the result of his very sensitive assignment in nuclear weapons, prevented his promotion to the ranks of general officer. Colonel Abel's last assignment was as the Commander of the US Army Financial Services Activity. This unit had the responsibility to insure payment and the financial operations for of up to 500,000 troops in time of war.

After leaving the Army, he became a financial analyst in the space and electronics industries. In 1969 he began a13 year career as a mid-level executive at the University of Pennsylvania and then at the Hahnemann Medical College and Hospital. In 1981, he was asked to return active duty to head the team redesigning the military pay system of the Army Reserve and National Guard.

In 1983, upon returning to civilian life, he became an officer of a 2-billion-dollar bank where he was in charge of the bank operations at over 50 locations. In 1985, Mr. Abel returned to education and was appointed Dean of Business Services at the Reading Area Community College. His last position was the chief operating officer for one of the largest school districts in Pennsylvania. During the more than 12 years he served as the chief operating officer of the Central Bucks School District, he built over $120 million of new schools in addition to running this rapidly growing school system.

Mr. Abel was active in politics in the 70's and served as a committee person and campaign chairman for the state legislator in his area. His biography appears in Who's Who in the World and Who's Who in Finance and he was certified for Federal Senior Executive Service positions.

He has written scores of articles that have been published throughout the country.

In 1998 he retired to Southwest Florida with Carol, his wife of 26 years. He is president of the Cape Coral Housing, Rehabilitation and Development Corporation, a nonprofit organization that provides low-income senior housing and helps low income homeowners repair their homes.

He served as Board Chairman of the Christ Lutheran Church School in Cape Coral, Florida. Mr. Abel has three children, three stepchildren and three grandchildren.

www.ingramcontent.com/pod-product-compliance
Lightning Source LLC
Chambersburg PA
CBHW061310280526
45784CB00002B/946